WHAT DO WE DO ABOUT

*What 44 Years of Ministry
Have Taught Me*

Dr. Joel A. Nelson

ISBN 979-8-89243-758-5 (paperback)
ISBN 979-8-89243-759-2 (digital)

Copyright © 2024 by Dr. Joel A. Nelson

All rights reserved. No part of this publication may be reproduced, distributed, or transmitted in any form or by any means, including photocopying, recording, or other electronic or mechanical methods without the prior written permission of the publisher. For permission requests, solicit the publisher via the address below.

Christian Faith Publishing
832 Park Avenue
Meadville, PA 16335
www.christianfaithpublishing.com

Printed in the United States of America

Contents

Introduction

No matter what people may think, feel, and say, Sunday school ministries are never going away. Not even a history-making, life-altering pandemic could change that.

As long as there are children, and then parents and churches wanting those children to learn moral values, spiritual truths, a Christian worldview, and the way to eternal life in Jesus, there will need to be Christ-centered ministries for children and youth. And as long as children, parents, and churches recognize the benefits and blessings of learning moral values, spiritual truths, a Christian worldview, and the way to eternal life in Jesus, side by side with others in a high quality, age-appropriate, organized, engaging, and caring environment, Sunday schools—or whatever name they take—will continue to serve a wonderful and valuable purpose.

This book is being written because I believe in Sunday schools. They are the Christian education ministry impacting the most children across the country, maybe even the world. I went to them. I taught in them. I supervised them. I championed them. I also saw the spiritual, mental, physical, and emotional good the Holy Spirit works through this timeless form of ministry. Some current statistics cast a gloomier shadow, but this data need not discourage.

People who study youth ministry trends have noted that Sunday school participation in America is going down. In the early 2000s, the Barna Group reported that America lost 20,000 Sunday school programs and that student enrollment had fallen across denominations. From 2004 to 2010, for example, Sunday school attendance dropped nearly 40 percent among Evangelical Lutheran churches in America and almost 8 percent among Southern Baptist churches, prompting speculation that the problem may be more than just a decline in American religiosity.[1] Barna suggested that churches no longer offering programming for children ages 2 to 5 (declining 94 percent to 88 percent), as well as those discontinuing junior high programs (dropping from 93 percent to 86 percent) were the catalyst for the attendance downturn.

Current data from the Lutheran Church Missouri Synod (LCMS) revealed that for congregations reporting their statistics, the average enrollment of youth ages 7 to 12 in Sunday school has declined by 35 percent over the past decade. For children ages toddler to grade 6, the decrease was 40 percent.[2] A statement from the Wisconsin Evangelical Lutheran Synod's (WELS) most recent *Book of Reports and Memorials* simply said this: "In the past decade Sunday school enrollment has experienced a sharp decline."[3]

Is this decline because there are fewer children in America? Nope. Data from *Childstats* reveals that the population of children infant to age 17 in the United States has grown from 64.2 million in 1990 to 74.3 million today.[4] So what's the deal? It might be that parents and kids don't see the Sunday school programs being offered them as worth their precious time. They actually may be interested but just not in the way it's being delivered.

What do we do about Sunday school? How can we change things and turn around the negative trends? How can we improve and increase Sunday school's place for kids and families? This book is a shot at answering these questions. God willing, it hits the mark.

Part 1

Who Am I?

Call me...*retired.*

I decided in high school literature class that if I ever wrote anything "big," it would begin like Herman Melville's *Moby Dick.*[5] I thought Melville's beginning was simple, to the point, and memorable. God willing, this book will meet the same standard, but with hundreds of pages to spare! Sidebar: I also thought starting a book "In the beginning..." would be cool, but I can't compete with that author.

I am indeed retired after forty-four years of "church work" in seven different positions/calls in Christian churches, schools, and national offices.[6] Each position/call was unique in many ways, stretching and growing my skills, faith, and ministry philosophy. They blessed me with exposure to a diversity of ages, ethnicities, socioeconomic demographics, geographic locations, and levels of corporate ministry. These positions/calls also motivated me to continue my education, resulting in a master's degree in family studies and a doctorate in leadership for the advancement of learning and service.[7]

Though my ministry was diverse, there was a universal thread. Every place I served, I was also involved with Sunday school in one way or another: teacher, superintendent, youth ministry director, national church-body executive providing services and support, and always an advocate. I have learned things that can be helpful to oth-

1

ers. I'm not comfortable being called an expert, but I have experienced and studied a lot on the subject. I know stuff. You'll have to decide how much of my stuff becomes your stuff.

Who Are You?

The first thing I can say about you, other than I have no clue who you are, is that you are curious. Something has moved you to pick up this book. I know it's not because of my history, ministry reputation, intellect, or great faith. You are curious because you feel something about Sunday school. You are a past student or current student, a past or current teacher, a Sunday school leader, a parent, or perhaps a pastor. You might even be a person wondering why this book was included in the $2 bundle you bought at your neighborhood garage sale. Whatever your status, suffice it to say, curiosity has gotten you this far. I'd also like to think your curiosity is fueled by a belief that there's something about Sunday school that's important, worthwhile, valuable, and timely.

A quick definition. Throughout this book, I use the term *Sunday school* because it's easier. I use the term *Sunday school* because it seems to be universally understood. I believe, however, other names are better and can communicate more clearly the purpose and place for this form of youth ministry.

Sunday schools developed as helpful vehicles to educate children. They were originally literacy schools where poor children could learn to read, using the Bible as the textbook. During the Industrial Revolution, many children spent all week (Monday–Saturday) working in factories. Christian philanthropists wanted to free these children from a life of illiteracy. Sunday was the only available time to do it.

Over time, and with the advent of child labor laws, nonworking days, public education, secular subjects, new textbooks, church-state separation, etc., Sunday school became a church-only and solely Christian education ministry. Still targeted at children, preschool to teenage, it frequently remained on Sunday mornings, reduced to an hour or so to coincide with worship services and/or adult Bible classes.

Today, Sunday school ministries have developed other names and different approaches because their purpose has changed. Sunday schools today are a place to increase Bible knowledge, learn the language of the church, study Christian doctrine, grow faith through the power of the Holy Spirit, develop and deepen a relationship with Jesus Christ and other believers, appropriate a Christian worldview, and learn how to spread the Good News, but in a more engaging, kid-friendly way.

A name change is helpful because some Sunday schools meet on days other than Sunday and/or do not want to come across as another day of school, aka boring and bothersome. On this point, Cynthia Tobias, nationally recognized Christian speaker, author, and educator said,

> When it comes to teaching Sunday School, a lot of times I'll ask groups of Sunday School teachers, "By and large with the children in your church, if they go especially to a public high school or a public elementary school, does school make them feel valued? Does it make them feel loved? Does it make them feel understood?" Well, usually the answer is, "No, it really doesn't." School is kind of, for a lot of kids, a prison sentence. So, on Sunday, if I come to church, do I want another day of school? That's the last thing I want! If there was one oasis in the whole week of school for kids who aren't very happy about learning, shouldn't it be the time when you step into that church, into that place of worship and finally feel understood, finally feel valued, instead of saying, "Sit still. Be quiet. Finish your work sheet. Memorize that verse." I want to know what is the point of my coming to church if it's just like school and, if I could quickly get out of school as soon as I can,

wouldn't I also look forward to the time when I no longer have to come to church? [Sunday school] needs to be a place I want to come to, I feel understood, I understand that that's what it's all about.[8]

Tobias's words give us a lot to think about. Are our Sunday school classrooms places to which our students want to come, where they feel valued and understood? Are they a weekly oasis that makes a positive difference for children who come from a lot of different places physically, economically, socially, intellectually, emotionally, and spiritually? God willing, we answer these questions in one of two ways: "Yes, they are!" or "No, they're not, but we're working like crazy to make them this way!"

To achieve Tobias's vision, you need a lot more than a name change. It's what's inside that counts. A simple name change can help to communicate, however, that your Sunday school is different, special, worth your time, and cool.

Google "other names for Sunday school," and hundreds of options appear: Kids Club, Jesus's Kids, JAM (Jesus and Me) Sessions, Classmates for Christ, Victory Kids, Power Hour, Truth Seekers, Prospectors, and scores more. These name changes are wonderful and help to communicate that Sunday school will be more like Jesus might have done it: engaging, interactive, memorable, inclusive, caring, faith-nurturing, and fun. Hey, how about "Funday School"? Maybe not.

So, if curiosity alone has gotten you to read to this point, *praise the Lord*! My prayer, however, is that you are seeking some deeper insights and will keep reading and learning more about one of the absolute best Christian education ministries for children there is. God willing, you'll see that Sunday school is indeed important, worthwhile, valuable, and timely. God willing, you'll also see a bigger, better place for yourself in it.

Part 2

What Do You See?

Look at the multicolored image on the front cover of this book. What is it trying to say? Look at it again. What thoughts come into your mind?

Here are my thoughts. First, the "good news." The image is kind of pretty. Abstract yet appealing. The words *Sunday School* floating atop the running-together splash and splotch of rainbow colors in a dance that says Sunday school is beautiful, creative, multifaceted, and dynamic. It says there are many parts and passions mixing toward something good yet undefined.

Here are more thoughts: the "bad news." The image is a big mess. It needs a do-over. The words *Sunday School* are fighting to stay topside on a color palette of chaos and disarray. A lot of potential but a lack of direction, emotional turbulence, and competing values are washing together toward a homogeny of worthlessness.

Okay, I'll admit those descriptions are a bit over the top. (Did I mention I liked creative writing in school?) The descriptions do, however, communicate realities all too present in Sunday school ministries. That multicolored image can trigger our minds and hearts to entertain new possibilities.

Most Sunday schools have *a lot* of beautiful/wonderful things going on but would benefit from more focus, direction, and guidance. They frequently have access to everything needed—human and material—to be truly awesome and successful but lack good processes and systems that maximize effort. Every Sunday school can paint a better picture of itself.

Let me also be very clear about this: Sunday school, like all other ministries of the Word of God, has God's power, guidance, and blessing on it when that Word is taught and used correctly and respectfully. God always accomplishes what he wants through his Word.[9] Sunday school advancement and success in any Christian church is God's doing, not ours. We dare not take the credit for God's work. We also, however, must not become what Lutheran professor and author Rev. David Kuske called "a roadblock for the Holy Spirit."[10] What we do and how we do it makes a huge difference.

In the next sections, let's explore how Sunday schools can become better. Let's answer these three questions:

- Why do we care about Sunday school?
- What do we want Sunday school to be?
- How do we make a quality Sunday school happen?

Part 3

Why Do We Care About Sunday School?

Take a few moments to think about the above question. Before reading on, jot down a couple of answers.

Why do we care about Sunday school? As I have reflected on that question over the years and discussed it with other ministry practitioners and theorists, these four answers emerged:

1. Eternal souls are at stake.
2. It's *the* opportunity for many.
3. It's a great way to serve.
4. It works.

Let's explore each answer a little more.

Why Do We Care About Sunday School?

1. Eternal Souls Are at Stake

Ever heard of W. C. Fields? Wikipedia says, "William Claude Dukenfield, better known as W. C. Fields, was an American comedian, actor, juggler, and writer. Fields's comic persona is a misanthropic and hard-drinking egotist who remained a sympathetic character despite his supposed contempt for children and dogs."[11] The line I remember most from a W. C. Fields film was this: "Beat it, kid, you bother me!"[12]

"Beat it, kid, you bother me!" was basically what Jesus's disciples said in Mark 10:13–16[13] when a bunch of parents who "got it" wanted Jesus to touch and bless their offspring. Jesus didn't like his disciples' approach at all. He was indignant! Jesus's ministry and his message were a whole new way of looking at things. Jesus elevated the status of children and the women who bore them. It was abundantly clear. To Jesus, kids' lives—temporal and spiritual—matter. Jesus came to save children too. Their eternal souls are at stake.

Kids' lives matter. The Great Commission,[14] Jesus's marching orders to the church, define and amplify the task at hand and until the end of time: make disciples, baptize, teach everyone—all nations. This includes children. Martin Luther, in his *Small Catechism*, notes that the Bible is clear on this point.[15] Children believe in Jesus and their eternal souls are precious.

The most quoted youth ministry Bible passage (Proverbs 22:6 NIV: "Start children off on the way they should go, and even when they are old they will not turn from it.") connects the spiritual training of children to a long life of focus and purpose. We train children in the truth of the Bible because it helps them successfully navigate life on earth. More importantly, it leads them to heaven. We care about Sunday school because the Holy Spirit uses the Bible training it provides to save our kids. *We care about Sunday school because eternal souls are at stake.*

2. It's *the* Opportunity for Many

What do you think the diagram below is trying to illustrate?

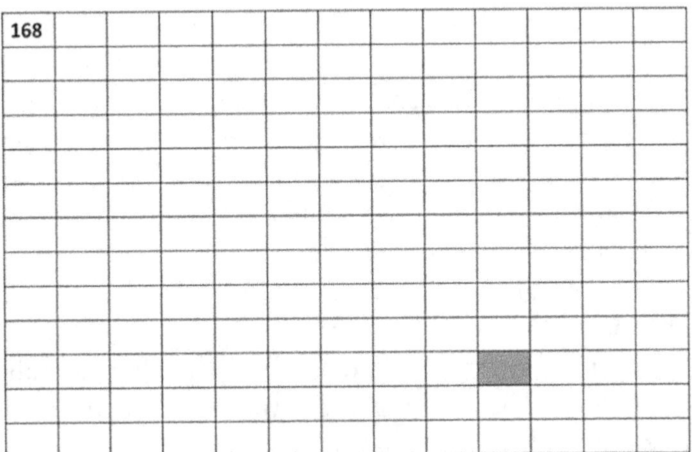

If you skew more left-brained linear in your thinking, you have already counted the number of boxes, 168. Hence the "clue" in the top left box. Now, how many hours are in a week? 24 × 7 = 168. Next, see that one box is shaded in. That stands for one hour (brilliant, no?)—one hour out of the whole week, 1/168. This diagram represents the amount of time many children (and families) dedicate to religious training: one hour a week. If you include church with Sunday school, you could expand the weekly Christian education duration to perhaps two hours.

One to two hours out of 168! The point is obvious. In any given week, many children have sparse contact with God's Word. Sunday school may be *the* only opportunity they get to learn about Jesus. Getting into why that is, is a whole new writing assignment (hmm… call me *author*?).

The weekly time-crunch competition Sunday schools and families face presents a huge challenge. Sadly, many Sunday schools don't meet it. Christian researcher George Barna once wrote, "Christian education opportunities for adults and children simply do not provide the quality of teaching and experience that people demand these days in exchange for their time."[16] Leaders in the church may be peeved by the perceived priorities parents have and the weekly choices they make, but leaders ignoring the "Why?" and the "How come?" of these choices is not helpful at all and possibly even sinful.

The Christian education choices families make for their children may have less to do with them and everything to do with the Christian education options given them. Peter Benson and Carolyn Eklin of Search Institute spoke to this well when they wrote, "Christian education in a majority of congregations is a tired enterprise in need of reform. Often out of touch with adult and [youth] needs, it experiences increasing difficulty in finding and motivating volunteers, faces general disinterest among its 'clients,' and employs models and procedures that have changed little over time."[17]An "out of the mouths of babes" nugget came from third grader Ben, when he told publisher, editor, and author Thom Schulz exactly why he did not want to be at Sunday school: "The teachers just talk, and we just sit there."[18]

Some years ago, at our last Sunday school class of the year, I passed out pens and paper and asked my seventh-grade students to respond to this question: "If you could design a Sunday school class / classroom / class period, what would it look like?" Here is a representative sampling of what they wrote (Full disclosure: I thought I was already doing a pretty good job!):

- "I would want to make students closer to Jesus and to each other. It would be more than just a Bible story. I would be getting the kids very involved and making them think."
- "Get all the kids involved with writing on the board, games, and other things for kids to participate."
- "Use games, videos, computers in our lessons."
- "I would have it be fun and exciting so people would want to come back and learn about God all the more. I would have a classroom filled with cool activities."
- "I would play some contemporary and some traditional Christian songs. I would teach the lesson the first week and then have a video to review the lesson the second week. If I did not use a video, I'd use games that related to the lesson."

These are more "out of the mouths of babes" evidence affirming that we must make our Sunday school classes and ministries better.

Sunday school must be the absolute best, highest quality, most meaningful, and most memorable possible. We will get only a small shot at it. That shot needs to hit the bull's-eye.

We must guarantee that our Sunday school ministry is top-notch. We want kids to come back. We want kids (and their parents) to feel Sunday school is totally worth their time. Most of all, we want to bring glory to God!

In his book *Bringing Out the Best in People*, Christian author and psychologist Dr. Alan Loy McGinnis expresses that the vast majority of people want things better. He writes that there is no such thing as an unmotivated person: "People do not like being lethargic and bored. They will welcome the manager who can teach them to enjoy their work, or the teacher who will impart to them a love of learning that causes the school day to go swiftly."[19] It's the same with Sunday school.

Everyone wants to be connected to a winner. Jesus is the ultimate and perfect Winner. He defeated sin, death, and hell. A top-notch Sunday school ministry, doing all things to the glory of God,[20] in a decent and orderly way,[21] and trusting that the Holy Spirit is leading it can bring more and more children to Jesus, the Winner Everlasting. A truly "winning" Sunday school ministry can be just the thing that moves kids and parents to recalibrate their weekly calendar.

Please note well: I fully understand and doggedly believe that the Holy Spirit is doing the heaviest lifting in this effort. We are only his conduits. But as noted earlier, we dare not become roadblocks. What we do and how we do our Sunday school ministry has a huge impact. No one will ever sway me from that perspective.

The Sunday school hour may very well be 1/168 of a child's weekly experiences. We need to make it the absolute best and most meaningful hour. *We care about Sunday school because it's the opportunity for many.*

3. It's a Great Way to Serve

There are several ways people become involved with Sunday school:

- The pastor asked me and I said, "Yes." After all, he's the… you know…pastor!
- I responded to a plaintive, after-church announcement, "Unless we get five more volunteers to join the Sunday school staff, Jesus's little lambs will not be able to experience the amazing wonders of God's grace, and 75 years of tradition at St. Barnabas will end."
- I lost a bet with the chairman of the church council. End of story.
- I only wanted a little more information to help me decide, but I got a Sunday school teacher's manual, calendar of lessons for the year, a student attendance chart, schedule of staff meetings, volumes 1 and 2 of *Kretzmann's Popular Commentary of the Bible*, and a key for the classroom!
- My great-grandmother, grandmother, and mother were Sunday school teachers here. Who am I to buck tradition? You know what? They are all still teaching.
- My dad is the chairman of the Christian Education Committee, for cryin' out loud!
- I really wanted to help…no kidding…honest…why are you looking at me that way?

Whether silly or serious, there are many ways people become involved in Sunday school. Getting good volunteers and qualified helpers is frequently tough sledding. We'll explore *how* to get people involved in an upcoming section. In this section, we focus on *why* helping with Sunday school is a great way to serve.

God uses all kinds of people in his church to advance his kingdom. The cavalcade of good, bad, and ugly characters in Bible history makes this very clear. In today's church, many examples could be given of people who were asked to serve in some capacity—even if they weren't totally gifted for it—and yet got the job done. God keeps working it out. For the purposes of this topic, however, let's assume that all Sunday school volunteers and helpers have these simple attributes: they love Jesus, like children, aren't intimidated by them, and are conscientious, dedicated, reliable, organized, willing, and positive. *Why* is helping with Sunday school a great way for these folks to serve? At the highest level, helping with Sunday school is being like Jesus.

Evangelist D. L. Moody[22] told a story about a picture he had seen that impressed him greatly. The picture portrayed a woman grasping a cross with both hands as she was being rescued from a stormy sea. Moody would then tell how that picture lost much of its impact after he saw another picture. In the second picture, a woman was also being rescued from raging waters. But while clinging with one hand to the cross, her other hand was lifting another person out of the waves to safety.

That second picture dramatically portrays what we who have been rescued from the penalty of our sins should be doing. We should be recognizing that others around us are in deep, raging spiritual trouble and in need of our help. We should be reaching out to them, stretching out serving hands in order to draw these people closer to the Gospel, closer to Jesus, so he can heal and save them.

Teaching/helping with Sunday school is a great way to serve because you (not holy angels who could do it better) are lifting and leading people to Jesus, the Great Healer and Savior. What a privilege! What an honor! And when the people you are leading are children and youth, you have the personal, spiritual satisfaction of knowing you are an anti–W. C. Fieldsian disciple. You are following Jesus's all-knowing, all-loving injunction to "let the children come!"

Martin Luther King Jr. said, "Life's most persistent and urgent question is, 'What are you doing for others?'"[23] Teaching Sunday school is an incredible service to others, especially parents. You are partnering with them and the Holy Spirit to bring up their children in the training and instruction of the Lord. You are partnering with them and the Holy Spirit to introduce and establish the Christian worldview in their children. You are partnering with them and the

Holy Spirit to reveal that the benefits of knowing, loving, and living for Jesus are out of this world…literally!

Rick Warren, founder and senior pastor of Saddleback Church in California and author of *The Purpose-Driven Life* (and a lot of other things), takes it even further. He says, "The only way you can serve God is by serving other people."[24] This statement at first pass seems to discount the contributions of people who serve in a more behind the scenes, under the radar, "not directly interacting with people" role. That interpretation of Warren's words would be incorrect and inconsistent with what he says other places. Any service in the church directly or indirectly serves and impacts people as it ultimately serves and brings glory to God.

Being a part of a Sunday school ministry is a great way to serve because it gives volunteers an opportunity and avenue to use their individual God-given gifts in a fulfilling way. God tells us to use the talents and spiritual gifts he gives us.[25] God promises blessings when we do so.[26] One of the fruits/gifts of the Spirit is joy.[27] Serving brings joy.

Rabindranath Tagore was a Bengali writer, poet, painter, playwright, composer, and philosopher. In 1913, he became the first non-European to win the Nobel Prize in Literature. Tagore once penned these words: "I slept and dreamt that life was joy. I awoke and saw that life was service. I acted and behold, service was joy."[28] Ralph Waldo Emerson, an American essayist, lecturer, philosopher, abolitionist, and poet, wrote, "It is one of the most beautiful compensations of life, that no man can sincerely try to help another without helping himself."[29]

Tagore and Emerson were not Christians by a long shot, yet they realized how personally rewarding service to others can be. Though unacknowledged and unrealized by them, the natural knowledge of God, the imprint of the real and only God in them, moved them to see and personally feel something very good when service to others is done. Serving brings joy. Serving God as the main motivation for serving others brings divine joy. You can hear it in the following "sound bites" from Sunday school teachers I have worked with:

- Being a Sunday school teacher was definitely not on my list of things to do. I had a five-year-old who was going to be starting Sunday school and a two-year-old at home. As I went to drop my five-year-old off at Sunday school, the tears were running down her face, and she didn't want me to go. She was pulling on my heartstrings as kids will do, but it worked. The Holy Spirit used this, and the rest is history. I stayed with her that day and every Sunday after her first year. She is now thirty-four years old, and I have been teaching Sunday School for twenty-nine years. It has been such a blessing to me, I love children and want them to know their Savor. (Vicky)

- Teaching Sunday school was really fulfilling when former students would see me and remember things about class. It also brought me joy and a sense of true purpose over the years to teach full sets of siblings about Jesus. (Kurt)

- My favorite part about teaching Sunday school is hearing the kids' expressions of faith, having them share their personal meaning of the lesson. It makes me happy to know they are learning about Jesus, the Holy Spirit is working in them, and regardless of whatever happens during the week, they are pausing and spending time hearing about their Savior. There are many weeks where I learn something new from the lesson as we apply it to our lives, so my faith is strengthened as well! (Lisa)

- I highly encourage teaching. It's been a joy-filled honor of mine to help our church family. (Dave)

- Helping out with Sunday school helped me strengthen my relationship with God and my faith, and I was able to use my own faith to strengthen the faith of others as well. I also gained perspectives from other leaders' experiences, which helped me grow my Christian network and knowledge. Helping with Sunday school was also a great way to serve the church as I was able to volunteer my free time in a way that helped a whole community of fellow worshippers. Teaching in Sunday school brought me joy and fulfillment because I was able to teach young minds the Word of the Lord in an engaging and exciting way. Not only did this allow me to understand how children learn best and how to continue to nourish their Christian spirit, but it also helped strengthen my own connection with God every week. The Sunday school environment was always collaborative and inviting, something I looked forward to being a part of. (Kimmy)

More testimonials could be added, but the point is made: helping with Sunday school is a great way to serve, and this service brings great joy.

The joy of serving in Sunday school should not be limited to adults. Sunday school ministry is an excellent vehicle for bringing the perspective, potential, and place of teens into the church as well. Researcher Bret Goodman writes, "[Teens] frequently complain that, after confirmation, there is nowhere to go. There is the feeling that young people are not taken seriously, have no meaningful input, and play no significant role…more needs to be done to provide avenues for involvement."[30]

Thom Rainer adds, "Youth are not looking for freedom [from the church]; they desire responsibility…each church has the responsibility to make them a valued part of ministry."[31]

George Barna reported, "Research reveals that adult church leaders usually had serious involvement in church life and training when they were young…the individuals who will become the church's leaders two decades from now are probably active in church programs today."[32]

When my oldest daughter, Natalie, was in high school, she rarely missed getting up on Sunday mornings to be at church. And her parents never had to remind her. I know, I know, teens getting up on their own for Sunday morning church seems astonishing, but Natalie did it. Her reason: "My babies are counting on me." Natalie's "babies" were the kids in her preschool Sunday school class. This Sunday morning situation created a real win-win-win.

The children won. They learned about their Savior and serving him from a creative, caring, and cool older youth who knew Jesus too. Those kids loved "Miss Natalie," and she loved them…tons.

Natalie won. She explored using her God-given gifts, abilities, and faith at a time when you're wrestling with self-esteem, identity, and purpose on top of questioning if spiritual things and "church" make any difference. Every Sunday morning, Natalie had over a dozen little reasons to feel valued, fulfilled, focused, and confident. She had the affirmation and appreciation of her students' parents, fellow teachers, and the congregation. Best of all, Natalie had real-world proof that this "Jesus stuff" has a real-life impact. Natalie better understood what Paul was saying to young Timothy, "Don't let anyone look down on you because you are young, but set an example for the believers in speech, in conduct, in love, in faith and in purity" (1 Timothy 4:12). Helping with Sunday school—and all that went into it—was a big reason that teen Natalie went on the become a full-time Christian teacher.

Finally, parents won. My wife and I proudly watched our teen grow in faith and skills and did not have to engage in the classic Sunday-morning adolescent versus adult confrontation conversation:

MOM: (With gentle purpose, peeking into teen son's dark room.) "Honey, time to get up for church." (Repeated at least three times while gingerly crossing the room to open window blinds a bit.)

TEEN: (Grumbling while rolling over and covering head to avoid light.) "I'm sleeping in."

MOM: (Loving but serious) "Come on, sweetheart, you know church is important."

TEEN: (Annoyance and volume rising…still under covers) "Says who?"

DAD: (Loud, with emphasis…passing bedroom door) "I do! And so does God."

TEEN: (Removes covers from head, squinting, and turns to door) "God wants me to rest on the seventh day, just like he did."

MOM: "Don't get spicey."

TEEN: (Plaintively) "I was out until after midnight."

DAD: (Louder with sarcastic irritation from nearby kitchen) "Too bad, so sad. Jacob wrestled all night, blew out his hip, and still got up to pray to God and seek his blessing. Get up. We leave in twenty-two minutes."

Alternate ending 1: Teen reluctantly gets up, makes half effort to get ready, goes to church, and angrily simmers in the pew while battling his head's vertical pendulum effect and smelling his own unbrushed teeth breath.

Alternate ending 2: Teen never gets up, even though Mom physically stops Dad from charging into the room and lighting Junior's bed on fire. Mom and Dad go to church but are annoyed, defeated, and distracted. Son is still in bed, snoring sinfully when parents arrive home ninety-seven minutes later.

No matter who you are or how old you are, Sunday school involvement can bring with it some awesome outcomes. *We care about Sunday school because it's a great way to serve.*

4. It Works

Let's review. Why do we care about Sunday school? We have considered these reasons: (1) eternal souls are at stake, (2) it's *the* opportunity for many, and (3) it's a great way to serve. Let's look at the fourth and perhaps most important reason: it works.

A 1959 *Christianity Today* cover story asked, "Shall We Close the Sunday School?" In answer, the article shared this: "Though the Sunday School seems to limp along, it often accomplishes wonders. Only an all-wise God could utilize untrained volunteers, meager physical facilities, and limited materials to change the course of so many lives."[33] What was true about Sunday school in the past is still true today. Sunday school and the good news of Jesus it proclaims changes the course of people's lives. It accomplishes its mission to bring people to heaven. It works. What God does always works.[34]

Consider the following:

Item #1: A great Sunday school draws in parents. Without parent interest, permission, and cooperation, you don't get the kids. One of the key findings of *Guiding Children to Discover the Bible, Navigate Technology & Follow Jesus*, a Barna Group research effort, revealed that over half (58 percent) of highly engaged

Christian parents acknowledged children's programming was the primary reason they chose their current church. The report said, "Even though children may be small, they carry big weight when it comes to family decisions about where to worship."[35]

Item #2: Sunday school involvement as kids helps people stay connected to the church when adults. Barna again provides some detail: "When it comes to church engagement, those who attended Sunday school or other religious programs as children or as teens were much more likely than those without such experiences to attend church and to have an active faith as adults." Looking at the data from the other side found that the highest proportion of unchurched adults was found among those who had never attended as children or teenagers. Barna writes, "Weekly activity as a child and weekly or monthly activity as a teen were connected with the lowest levels of disconnection from church attendance."[36]

Item #3: Barna's research on youth and the church revealed another wonderful outcome. He writes, "Children who are most active in church [like in Sunday school] tend to engage with the Bible outside of church, to attend church activities other than Sunday worship (such as Bible studies, camps, or children's/youth events), and to pray together with their family as well. They are also about twice as likely to engage in outreach activities and volunteerism, demonstrating that the level of dedication in this group to the overall mission of the church is not only internally focused, but expresses itself in outward action."[37]

Now George Barna is just one researcher, but his reputation is solid. He and his research organization are extremely credible. I believe what he finds. If pressed, more results from other sources could also be found to affirm the claims. The biggest reason I'm convinced of the data above, however, is because I've seen all of it with my own eyes.

After four-plus decades of ministry with youth and families myself, I could recount many examples where the items above happened. The Holy Spirit was definitely at work, the gospel of Jesus was changing hearts in children and parents, and Sunday school was the vehicle through which both were happening.

Perhaps the best way to affirm that Sunday school does indeed "work" for children and families would be to hear from benefactors themselves. Here's what some parents said:

- [Sunday school] became the foundation we have built on to raise up our children in Christ. We have been able to make [it] a priority for our family, and it also has led to us attending church and receiving communion regularly. It has strengthened our family spiritually and serves as an incredible resource for fellowship and support. It truly is invaluable. Finally, as parents, it grants us a lot of peace knowing that our kids are surrounded by those who share their faith and can assist to grow it, especially since they attend public school. (Megan and Travis)

- I teach three-year-old Sunday school. My class is sometimes the first introduction to a "school" setting. We teach the kids the stories of Creation through Ascension. It's so exciting to hear the parents tell me that their child was telling them all about the lesson throughout the week and couldn't wait to come the next Sunday. Parents and children alike will pass me years later in the hall and still refer to me as Miss Vicky. They'll also recall something their children still remember from class. Sunday school has a real impact, and I am so glad God gave me the ability and opportunity to teach his word and spread his love. (Vicky)

- The experiences of my children in Sunday school are the bedrock of our church, faith, and family. The lessons are sound and activities keep the kids interested. My children would always be talking about the lesson on the way home and often singing the songs. They have a firm spiritual foundation because of Sunday school. I highly encourage it for all church families. (David)

- [Sunday school] has been so important for us as a family. We value the opportunity that this gives our kids to study

God's word at their level, pray, sing in church, and grow in God. Our kids don't have God's word in their school, and we really need a church that cares about the growth of our children. It makes a big difference when we are included in activities and given the opportunity to interact with other church families. We as parents pick a church for the opportunities our children have to grow in God. I know many churches focus on the older congregation members, but it is so important to provide the children a solid foundation in God's Word. The church also has the responsibility to love the children and give them an opportunity to grow in God. I truly value that [our church] through its Sunday school gives children the opportunities to grow in God's Word. It means so much to us and our kids. (Kristin)

Here are some responses from children who wrote notes to me as part of the Sunday school's celebrating my last session before retirement. Most kids did not include their names and were not "coached" on what to write.

- Thanks for leading [Sunday school]. It is awesome! I like bringing my friends to it too.
- I love [Sunday school] because I learn about Jesus in a fun way. I love you too!
- You know I have been coming to [Sunday school] my whole life (pre-K to sixth grade). It has made my faith strong. I know Jesus is my Savior and best friend. Thanks!
- [Sunday school] taught me a lot about the Bible in a way that I remember. I love coming and pray you will have a good retirement.
- I went to [Sunday school] for all the years it was offered and then joined the [Sunday school] staff. I have grown so much in my faith and love helping other kids grow too.
- [Sunday school] rocks! I loved the songs and activities about our lessons and Jesus.

Sunday school accomplishes so much. It draws families, parents, and kids into the church so they can be exposed to the good news of Jesus. Involvement in Sunday school when young dramatically increases the likelihood that people will remain connected to the church through life. Sunday school helps bring focus and meaning to families. Faith nurtured by the Holy Spirit through Sunday school expresses itself in places and ways outside of it. Sunday school participation makes kids and adults happy. *We care about Sunday school because it works!*

Part 4

What Do We Want Sunday School to Be?

In the preceding sections, the question, "Why do we care about Sunday school?" was given a four-part answer: (1) Eternal souls are at stake. (2) It's *the* opportunity for many. (3) It's a great way to serve. (4) It works.

In this section, an equally important question will be explored: "What do we want Sunday school to be?"

A pastor was giving the children's message during church. For this part of the service, he would gather all the children around him and give a brief lesson. On this particular Sunday, he was using squirrels for an object lesson on industry and preparation. He started out by saying, "I'm going to describe something, and I want you to raise your hand when you know what it is." The children nodded eagerly.

"This thing lives in trees (pause) and eats nuts (pause)…" No hands went up. "It's gray (pause) and has a long, bushy tail (pause)…" The children were looking at each other, but still no hands raised. "And it jumps from branch to branch (pause) and chatters and flips its tail when excited (pause)…"

Finally, one little boy tentatively raised his hand. The pastor breathed a sigh of relief and called on him. "Well…" began the boy, "I know the answer is Jesus…but it sure sounds like a squirrel to me!"

A cute little story. Sometimes the punch line, however, is the inside joke in many church circles. The answer to almost every religious question is either "Jesus" or "sin."

In all honesty, these two words give us the simplest answer to the question, "What do we want Sunday school to be?" Sunday school is a place where we teach kids about Jesus, their sins, and how Jesus took away their sins. That's the amazing grace salvation story, and that's truly the preeminent purpose for any Christian education ministry.

To stop our thinking there, however, prevents us from considering some other really helpful ideas. Consider this question: is Sunday school a place where kids learn about Jesus, or is it a place where kids experience Jesus? Take a couple of moments to reflect on that. Really thinking about both parts of that question can help us determine what we want Sunday school to be.

Sunday school is a place where kids learn about Jesus.

This statement is totally true. For me, it also includes the ideas of being more formal and more cognitive. The purpose is to get children to know the Bible and the story of salvation with facts, spiritual truths, biblical chronologies, points of doctrine, and proof passages. Kids "sit and soak." The *school* part of Sunday school seems to pop out with this statement. That's not wrong; it's just there.

Sunday school is a place where kids experience Jesus.

This statement is totally true too. For me, it also includes the ideas of being more interactive, relational, and hands-on. The purpose is to get children to know the Bible and the story of salvation. How they fit in and how it applies to life. They talk about it and work with it. Kids learn side by side with Christian friends and teachers, all the while getting to know their best Friend and Savior, Jesus, and everything he's done for them and the world. As a result, a desire to "seek and serve" emerges.

After four decades of working in, with, and around Sunday schools and ruminating on best practices and how to raise the bar, I have come to believe that Sunday schools should be more so places where kids experience Jesus rather than just learn about him. Again, both parts of this dichotomy have value.

For me, the superior approach and philosophy is to "experience Jesus," especially for children from preschool through junior high ages. "Learn about Jesus" is perhaps more age-appropriate and better incorporated as a confirmation/church membership process where deeper Bible and doctrinal study is beneficial. Sunday school as a place where kids experience Jesus is also more consistent with how God created us.

Perhaps the most "Aha!" moment I ever had about Sunday school philosophy and best practice, about teaching and learning in general, came after reading 1 John 1:1. I had read this verse many times before but never caught it. The evangelist John declares, "That which was from the beginning, which we have heard, which we have seen with our eyes, which we have looked at and our hands have touched—this we proclaim concerning the Word of life" (NIV).

What does this passage have to do with experiencing Jesus and God's creative power in our making? What does it have to do with what we want Sunday school to be?

Skim through the passage again, and note (maybe even highlight) these words: *heard, seen, touched.* John tells everyone that what they learned from and about Jesus was done through three distinct God-given senses or dispositions: hearing, seeing, and touching. In teacher education speak, these are known as the three basic learning modalities or styles: auditory (hearing), visual (seeing), and kinesthetic (touching).

I had been teaching for a couple of decades before I made the obvious connection. John shows that Jesus taught his disciples and others in a sensory way. Jesus, the Master Teacher, connected with his students through their God-given learning styles: auditory, visual, and kinesthetic. Jesus made the Word of Life come to life in hands-on, interactive, and experiential ways—the absolute best approach for making preachers and teachers who were to "seek and serve" the lost.

Accepting and acting on this can really help us answer the question, "What do we want Sunday school to be?" It also informs how we can make Sunday school a place where kids truly experience Jesus.

Before moving on, let me comment about the idea of "experiencing" Jesus. This concept makes some church people uneasy. For some, "experiencing" Jesus suggests personal emotions, feelings, and decisions—things that are tainted by sin and constantly in flux. These emotions, feelings, and decisions, it is felt, supplant the truth that God's changeless Word and the Holy Spirit, working through that Word, are what's creating faith and driving faith development. For some, "experiencing" takes the spotlight for faith formation and nurture away from the perfect God and points it to the imperfect individual. This is not what I'm talking about.

When I say, "Making Sunday school a place where kids truly experience Jesus," I simply mean that we create a culture and practices that put the Holy Spirit first but then enable and encourage kids to actually work with and explore the Bible, use physical objects and materials, have interactive discussions with classmates, and consider real-life situations and applications. We ask the Holy Spirit to help us make the Word of Life come to life in hands-on, interactive, and experiential ways, just like Jesus did. The way we do this—the way Jesus did it—is to connect with students through their God-given learning styles: auditory, visual, and kinesthetic.

Another "Aha!" moment when it comes to appreciating the role of learning styles in Christian education came to me through a book written by Jody Capehart, *Touching Hearts, Changing Lives*. In this book, Capehart looks in a new way at the most famous, children's Christian education verse in the Bible, Proverbs 22:6 (NIV): "Start children off on the way they should go, and even when they are old they will not turn from it."

I was always taught and taught others that the point of this passage was spiritual. Because the book of Proverbs focuses on spiritual matters, it's most likely that the words "his way" in the passage refer to the way God wants the person to go. Rev. Roland Cap Ehlke, in his commentary on the book of Proverbs, says, "The verse, then, does contain a beautiful assurance. One's childhood training in the Bible is never entirely forgotten. It's always there as a reminder, a corrective, and a directive on the path to heaven."[37] This is an excellent way to remember the passage.

Jody Capehart's take on Proverbs 22:6 added some new insights for me. She writes, "The word *should* [in the passage] has another implication here… 'On the way they should go' is literally, 'according to the child's way'… This verse implies that parents and teachers should discern the individuality and special strengths that God has given each one."[38] My "Aha!" takeaway from Capehart's words was this: we need to teach people *the Way* (the good news of Jesus) in *the way* God has designed them to learn, in the way they should go according to their God-given learning styles. This seems to be what Jesus did.

In the past couple of decades, research on how the brain works and how people learn has grown exponentially. Dig into it a bit, and you are blown away by how fearfully and wonderfully we are made (Psalm 139:14),[39] especially in the cranial department. The research on learning and the brain can be simplified and easily applied to improving Sunday schools. Here is a super simplification that checks most of the Sunday school teaching boxes.

Unless there is some kind of sensory deficit, every human being learns using the three basic learning modalities or styles: auditory (hearing), visual (seeing), and kinesthetic (touching). It is believed that most people are strong in at least two of the styles. Some are strong in all three. Many people have a preferred learning style. No one is restricted to just one style. You can easily test this using the simple modality checklist below, developed by Cynthia Tobias.[40]

Modality Checklist

Directions: Place a checkmark by all the statements that strongly describe what you prefer. Then add all the checkmarks in each column and write that number on the TOTAL line at the bottom of each column. The higher the TOTAL, the stronger the modality.

Auditory	Visual	Kinesthetic
_____ I need to hear myself say it in order to remember it.	_____ I need to see an illustration of what I'm being taught before I understand it.	_____ I have difficulty sitting still for more than a few minutes at a time.
_____ I often need to talk through a problem aloud in order to solve it.	_____ I am drawn to flashy, colorful, visually stimulating objects.	_____ I usually learn best by physically participating in a task.
_____ I memorize best by repeating the information aloud or to myself over and over.	_____ I almost always prefer books that include pictures or illustrations with the text.	_____ I almost always have some part of my body in motion.
_____ I remember best when the information fits into a rhythmic or musical pattern.	_____ I look like I'm "daydreaming" when I'm trying to get a mental picture of what's being said.	_____ I prefer to read books or hear stories that are full of action.
_____ I would rather listen to a recording of a book than sit and read it.	_____ I usually remember better when I can actually see the person who's talking.	_____ I remember best when I can do something with the information.
TOTAL: _______	TOTAL: _______	TOTAL: _______

In any group of people, no matter the age, small group or large, all three learning styles will be present. If you test this (which I have), it's always true. What's also frequently true is that the dominant learning styles frequently break down into thirds: 1/3 of the people in the group are strong auditory learners, 1/3 are strong visual learners, and 1/3 are strong kinesthetic learners. Knowing this is a key to making Sunday school lessons and Sunday school, in general, something kids and parents want to be a part of. It enables us to tailor lessons to meet the learning needs of each child. When children's needs are met, they enjoy the experience and the Sunday morning parent/child dialogue flips from…Mom: (Pleading) "It's time to go to Sunday school. Come on, kids, let's go," to…Kids: (Cheering) "Mom, it's time to go to Sunday school! Come on, let's go!"

Understanding and applying learning styles research to our Sunday school teaching can be a real game changer and can be used to enhance any curriculum. While you may not know the individual preferred learning styles for your Sunday school students (unless you "test" them), you do know that your class will have all three learning styles represented each Sunday. Figuring out ways to accommodate and connect with your students' learning styles will help make the Word of Life come to life for your kids. It will also make teaching a lot more fun for you. The best part: it's pretty simple to accomplish.

The table below helps make the case.

The Learning Modalities of My Students

Style	Description	Teacher Questions
VISUAL LEARNERS	They learn best by seeing and watching. They need to create pictures in their "mind's eye." They use imagination extensively. They like to draw and doodle. They can get "lost" in thought. Sometimes they are accused of daydreaming.	Do I have some colorful pictures, images or objects that relate to the lesson? What could I write or draw on the regular/electronic whiteboard? Is my presentation of the lesson "colorful" enough so students can paint in their minds, clear pictures of the lesson details? How can I move around during the lesson or use my own body motions to add visual interest? Does the lesson include a reinforcement activity that's visual?
AUDITORY LEARNERS	They learn best by listening and talking. They need to hear what they learn. They respond to sounds in the lesson like the teacher's voice (changing tone, volume, pitch) or other sounds brought into the lesson (music, special effects). They need "thinking noise" (being able to hear themselves and others say words and phrases). Sometimes they are accused of being the class "chatterboxes."	How can I add special sounds/sound effects to the lesson? Is there a place where music or singing could be added? How will I use my voice in different ways? How can I add opportunities for students to repeat words/phrases out loud? Could I add some pair-sharing or smaller group discussions?

KINESTHETIC LEARNERS	They learn best by moving. Movement aids their memory. They need breaks / "switch-ups" in the lesson and opportunities to physically change position and touch/ manipulate objects. Sometimes they are accused of being fidgety or "wiggle worms."	Will my lesson have a couple of physical "breaks" built into it (stand up, look to your left/right, raise your hands, clap twice, move over here, pass this around, etc.)? Could students move to smaller groups? Could we role-play a part of the lesson? Is there an action Bible song I could add? Do I have an active reinforcement activity?

An encouragement: the more you work at accommodating your students' learning styles, the easier, more natural, and more routine it will become. Practice makes perfect. The curriculum you use may also provide good help. If not, you can easily insert your own. The imperative is to have/use teaching methods and lesson components *each* Sunday that touch *every* learner in the way God has gifted them to go. This becomes especially important if you have children who do not attend regularly.

Though rare, some lessons/weeks may not always lend themselves to easy accommodation ideas. Don't fret. Like in every other human endeavor, balance is the key. Some weeks, your lesson presentation may skew more visual; some weeks more kinesthetic, for example. That's okay. You won't fracture the faith development of your God-given charges. Remember, the Holy Spirit is always doing the heavy lifting. Just make sure your week-to-week-to-week lessons present a nice balance of accommodations for each learning style.

To this point, our answer to the question, "What do we want Sunday school to be?" has three parts:

1. We want Sunday school to be a place where kids learn about Jesus, their sins, and how Jesus took away their sins. It's a place that presents the amazing grace salvation story.

2. We want Sunday school to be a place where kids truly experience Jesus, where we create a culture and practices that put the Holy Spirit first but then help us make the Word of Life come to life in hands-on, interactive, and experiential/real-life ways, just like Jesus did.

3. We want Sunday school to be a place where lessons and activities effectively connect with students through their God-given learning styles: auditory, visual, and kinesthetic.

To close this section, we need to add another important part to our answer: (4) We want Sunday school to be a place where everyone feels loved.

For Christians engaged in Jesus-sharing ministries, the statement above (4) seems like a big "Duh!" Of course, we love everyone and want to show Jesus's love to everyone! Like any relationship, however, we need to work at this love. Sunday schools are filled with sinful people. Satan, the executive director of the "Where Sunday Schools Go to Die" movement, works hard to mess things up. While love should be the obvious language and care the abundant currency of our Sunday schools, sometimes kids and parents don't feel it. Sadly, it may not be their fault but ours.

The famous phrase, "I don't care how much you know until I know how much you care," applies here. If we want kids and parents to know and feel the unconditional love of Jesus in their lives, they will have to always see it in ours. If we don't show unconditional love to those we serve through Sunday school…

- Nothing we say will matter.
  First Corinthians 13:1 (NIV): "If I speak in the tongues of men or of angels, but do not have love, I am only a resounding gong or a clanging cymbal."

- Nothing we know will matter.
  First Corinthians 13:2a (NIV): "If I have the gift of prophecy and can fathom all mysteries and all knowledge…but do not have love, I am nothing."

- Nothing we believe will matter.
First Corinthians 13:2b (NIV): "If I have a faith that can move mountains, but do not have love, I am nothing."

- Nothing we give will matter.
First Corinthians 13:3 (NIV): "If I give all I possess to the poor…but do not have love, I gain nothing."

- Nothing we achieve will matter.
First Corinthians 13:3 (NIV): If I…give over my body to hardship that I may boast, but do not have love, I gain nothing."[41]

Modeling and maintaining an unconditional love Sunday school ministry can only be done if those running the Sunday school are personally growing in their own knowledge and appreciation of the unconditional love shown them in Jesus. Effective Sunday school leaders need to be regular Means of Grace (Word and sacrament) users.

Someone once put the benefits this way, "To get the full flavor of an herb, it must be pressed between the fingers, so it is the same with the Scriptures; the more familiar they become, the more they reveal their hidden treasures and yield their indescribable riches." Psalm 19:7–10 (NIV) is even better:

The law of the Lord is perfect, refreshing the soul.
The statutes of the Lord are trustworthy, making
    wise the simple.
The precepts of the Lord are right, giving joy to
    the heart.
The commands of the Lord are radiant, giving
    light to the eyes.
The fear of the Lord is pure, enduring forever.
The decrees of the Lord are firm, and all of them
    are righteous.

> They are more precious than gold, than much
>   pure gold;
> They are sweeter than honey, than honey from
>   the honeycomb.

What do we want Sunday school to be? In short, we want it to be a place that shows what Jesus did to save, with the methods Jesus used to teach, through the styles Jesus gave to learn, in the unconditional love Jesus was.

Part 5

How Do We Make a Quality Sunday School Happen?

It's not impossible. It's just a little involved. What we need to do to make quality Sunday schools is not that difficult (in my opinion). It just takes willingness, commitment, effort, and time.

What follows are things I believe make quality Sunday schools possible. Some may seem "out of reach" for you and your situation. My encouragement and prayer is that you consider all of them seriously and outside of your own situation. Do they make sense? If employed, would they make a Sunday school better? If they would, then seriously consider how you could implement them—in whole or part—within your Sunday school ministry. Be open-minded. Think positively. Remember, God is with you.

I believe working on what follows will make a huge difference, but improvement won't happen overnight. You have to stay at it. You have to commit yourself and your congregation to seeking and keeping the standards. When you do, you'll deliver a ministry that children, families, and volunteers will want to be a part of.

A Sunday school teacher decided to have her young class memorize one of the most quoted passages in the Bible, Psalm 23. She gave the youngsters a month to learn the chapter. Little Ricky was excited about the task, but he just couldn't remember the Psalm. After much practice, he could barely get past the first line. On the day that the kids were scheduled to recite Psalm 23 in front of the congregation, Ricky was so nervous. When it was his turn, he stepped up to the microphone and said proudly, "The Lord is my Shepherd, and that's all I need to know."

Amen, little Ricky! When it comes to matters of faith and our salvation, Ricky is right. The Lord is our Shepherd and Savior, and that's all we need to know. When it comes to how to run a quality Sunday school, however, "We teach Jesus, Jesus, only Jesus!" is not a good enough answer. While Jesus called many disciples by simply saying, "Follow me," he did not leave it there. It wasn't redemption by association and justification by osmosis. Jesus did things to illustrate his truths, demonstrate his love, showcase his power, and prove his authority over the universe. Jesus had a definite purpose, strategy, and method. When it comes to how we make quality Sunday schools happen, we, too, need to be intentional.

How do we make it happen? How do we make our Sunday schools the best they can possibly be and ones that bring glory to God in every way? Fervently praying to God for this general outcome is a great start. We must, however, add some specific petitions to our prayer and seek some unique outcomes that, if realized, can truly make a difference.

How Do We Make a Quality Sunday School Happen?

1. Adjust Your Attitude

Consider the familiar quotes below.

- It is our attitude at the beginning of a difficult task, which, more than anything else, will affect its successful outcome.
- It is your attitude, not your aptitude, that determines your altitude.
- A bad attitude is like a flat tire. If you don't change it, you'll never go anywhere.
- The only disability in life is a bad attitude.
- Right attitudes produce right actions.

- Your attitude is either the lock on or the key to the door of success.

Now add what the Bible says. It's even more compelling.

- "May the God who gives endurance and encouragement give you the same attitude of mind toward each other that Christ Jesus had" (Romans 15:5 NIV).
- "Whatever you do, work at it with all your heart, as working for the Lord, not for human masters" (Galatians 3:23 NIV).
- "In your relationships with one another, have the same mindset as Christ Jesus: Who, being in very nature God, did not consider equality with God something to be used to his own advantage; rather, he made himself nothing by taking the very nature of a servant, being made in human likeness. And being found in appearance as a man, he humbled himself by becoming obedient to death—even death on a cross!" (Philippians 2:5–8 NIV).
- "Do nothing out of selfish ambition or vain conceit. Rather, in humility value others above yourselves, not looking to your own interests but each of you to the interests of the others" (Philippians 2:3–4 NIV).
- "Whatever you do, work at it with all your heart, as working for the Lord, not for human masters" (Colossians 3:23 NIV).
- "Finally, brothers and sisters, whatever is true, whatever is noble, whatever is right, whatever is pure, whatever is lovely, whatever is admirable—if anything is excellent or praiseworthy—think about such things. Whatever you have learned or received or heard from me, or seen in me— put it into practice. And the God of peace will be with you" (Philippians 4:8–9 NIV).

It all starts with attitude—a good and godly one.

Read out loud to yourself the two statements below. What's the difference?

- We've got to have a Sunday school at our church.
- We get to have a Sunday school at our church.

I don't mean to split hairs here too much, but the very similar statements above showcase a totally different attitude. For me, the first statement speaks to obligation, doing what's required, checking a box. The second statement speaks to opportunity, doing something special, and appreciating a privilege. The first statement comes from the weary; the second from winners. In forty-plus years of working in, with, and around Sunday schools, I have seen both. To create and sustain a quality Sunday school, you need to have a winning attitude.

Remember what we said about winners in part 3 of this book? Everyone wants to be connected to a winner, and Jesus is the Winner Everlasting!

Over my decades of youth ministry work, I have discovered and sung many cool songs about Jesus. One of my favorites is this one. It is from a Concordia Publishing House VBS program. You can find a 2017 video remake of it here: https://vimeo.com/187702333. The song is appropriately called "Winners!" and expresses the attitude we should have in our Sunday schools.

> Refrain:
> Jesus Christ has won the victory!
> Praise God we're winners in him!
> Jesus Christ has won the victory!
> Praise God we're winners in him.
>
> Verse 1:
> Some days we feel like losers who never do things
> right;
> But Jesus, our big Brother, is with us in the fight!
> (Refrain)

Verse 2:
We all need God's forgiveness; we sin, it's sad but
    true.
That's why God sent a Savior to die for me and
    you. (Refrain)

Verse 3:
Because God says we're winners in Jesus Christ
    our Friend,
We love, and serve, and praise him with joy that
    will not end. (Refrain)

I have used this song scores of times with children, teens, and adults. It really brings to focus Who's doing what. It emphasizes that Jesus is our Savior, Brother, and Friend. It's a song that gets our attitude pointing in a happy, heavenly direction. Having that, the rest is so much easier.

A congregation with pastors, leaders, and people who have this winning attitude, motivated by the Spirit-given faith and appreciation that Jesus Christ has won the victory over sin, death, and hell and is fighting with us until the end, is the first step toward making a "winning" Sunday school ministry.

2. Leverage Good Leadership

Just like there are hundreds of quotes about attitude, there are thousands about leadership. In any meaningful endeavor, especially Sunday school, who's leading, modeling, and showing the way is crucial. Someone needs to be in charge, and this person(s) needs to understand what that means. Consider these quotes.

American essayist Ralph Waldo Emerson wrote, "Every great institution is the lengthened shadow of a single man [woman]. His [her] character determines the character of the organization."[42] Emerson was not a theologian. He might not have been a good leader either. He does, however, make a salient point: organizations look like their leaders.

Second World War British field marshal James Montgomery said leaders have, "the capacity and the will to rally men and women to a common purpose and the character which inspires confidence."[43] Montgomery believed that competent leaders can inspire others and encourage them to meaningful, collective action through their spirit and modeling.

Napoleon Bonaparte, who is considered one of the greatest military commanders in history, said, "A leader is a dealer in hope."[44] To Napoleon, being positive and forward-looking is vital.

Then there's King Solomon. In Proverbs 29:18 (NIV), the Holy Spirit inspired him to write, "Where there is no vision, the people perish." A leader needs to know where he's going and see what can be.

Finally, there's Andrew, Simon Peter's brother. In John 1:40, Andrew hears John the Baptist say that Jesus is the Lamb of God. Andrew follows Jesus and then finds his brother Simon, telling him, "We have found the Messiah (that is, the Christ)." Andrew takes Peter to Jesus. Andrew was a leader who wanted others to know Jesus, just like he did.

More could be mined from additional leadership quotes and examples, but the above sample gives us plenty of context as we consider how to improve our Sunday schools. To review: (1) Organizations look like their leaders. (2) Leaders inspire and encourage others through their spirit and modeling. (3) Leaders must be positive and joy-filled. (4) Leaders need vision. (5) Leaders know and share Jesus.

A high-quality Sunday school ministry must have leaders who understand that their contribution will create the culture, the "lengthened shadow," that makes the ministry meaningful and desirable to parents, children, and Sunday school staff members. These leaders understand that their character and competence will inspire and encourage the rest of the Sunday school family. They appreciate that the positivity and joy they exude will be contagious to everyone involved and make the ministry inviting. These leaders see where the Sunday School can go, realizing its great potential and pursuing it relentlessly. Finally, they live for Jesus and want others to know and live for him too.

Pie in the sky? Is finding Sunday school leaders like this a pipe dream with reality being far different? Can pastors and/or church boards tasked with overseeing Sunday school ministry identify, recruit, and train such people? Absolutely! If we (a) are serious about making our Sunday school the best it can be—a winner, (b) we accept that good Sunday school leadership is vital, and (c) we know that "Jesus, our big Brother, is with us in the fight!" then (d) we figure it out.

We figure it out! We move away from the easier, "find a nice Christian willing warm body" staffing philosophy and commit ourselves to a serious and prayerful search for the qualified person God sees us having for "such a time as this."[45] The person who can do the job or is willing to learn how to do the job. And when you truly know and believe in what you need, you'll be amazed at whom God helps you find.

3. Use the Correct Curriculum

Sunday school is so relevant. It's a Christian education enterprise through which we help children increase their Bible knowledge, learn the language of the church, study Christian doctrine, grow faith through the power of the Holy Spirit, develop and deepen a relationship with Jesus Christ and other believers, appropriate a Christian worldview, and learn how to spread the Good News. We want this all to be done in an engaging, kid-friendly way. The $100,000 question: what curriculum do we use to make this happen?

Here's a bubble-burster: no curriculum is going to give you everything exactly the way you need it and want it. That's just the nature of curriculum development, publishing priorities, denominational influence, local realities, and personal preference. You'll always need to tweak things—drop out this, beef up that. If you think back to part 4, however, you just might be able to "figure it out" here too:

- We want Sunday school to be a place that shows what Jesus did to save, with the methods Jesus used to teach, through the styles Jesus gave to learn, in the unconditional love Jesus was.

Here are some additional curriculum criteria:

1. Does the curriculum help students see what the Bible is and why it's so precious?
2. Does the curriculum present God's inspired and inerrant Word in its truth and purity?
3. Does the curriculum acknowledge the role of the Holy Spirit in faith creation?
4. Does the curriculum help students understand sin and grace, law and gospel?
5. Does the curriculum help students see the chronology and characters of the salvation story?
6. Does the curriculum provide clear truths for each lesson, what we want to learn from this lesson, and how these truths connect to Jesus?
7. Does the curriculum offer good examples of how the lessons apply to real life?
8. Does the curriculum provide good "helps" for teachers: lesson overview, lesson truth review, presentation helps, tips for engaging all three learning styles, teacher prayer, etc.?

Full disclosure: I believe Sunday school should focus its attention on Bible history and simple Christian doctrine flowing from the Bible history lessons. There certainly is a place for and great value in deeper doctrinal study, but let's be mindful of our audience. Sunday school should lay the foundation and leave its young students with a clear understanding of who Jesus is and what he did to save us.

If your particular denomination offers its own curriculum, that's awesome and very helpful. Make sure, however, that you use it in ways that truly engage your students so that the Word of Life truly comes to life for them in memorable and meaningful ways.

4. Favor a Winning Format

"And now a word of thanks to those who volunteered
in the Sunday school ministry this year."

I saw this funny cartoon years ago. The original caption said something different. For the purposes of this section, however, I modified it.

How could it be that volunteering with Sunday school could be such a frazzling experience? Think back to part 2 of this book and the "What Do You See?" section. You were asked to look at the colored cover of this book. Recall that the "bad news" about the cover picture said this: "The words *Sunday School* are fighting to stay topside on a color palette of chaos and disarray. A lot of potential but a lack of direction, emotional turbulence, and competing values are washing together toward a homogeny of worthlessness." If a Sunday school ministry looks anything close to that description, then it's easy to see how volunteers could have a bad hair year. If volunteers get little or no direction, orientation, training, and help with curriculum and materials, it's easy to see how one's coiffure could get confused (more on all of this in the next section). A proactive remedy to avert such frustration can be found in the Sunday school's format.

Through my own teaching/managing trials and errors, and through my work as a national church body executive serving and supporting over 1,200 Sunday schools, I have seen various formats employed for conducting weekly Sunday school. By format, I mean the structure in which the Sunday school is managed, classes configured, and lessons taught. The format can look different in places because of available space, the enrollment numbers, and the experience of the staff. The actual curriculum used plays a part too. No formats are wrong, and most curricula can be adapted for each format. You'll need to determine which format is the best vehicle for creating a winning Sunday school ministry in your setting.

There are basically three formats used in Sunday schools: traditional, stations, and large group / small group. Here's a quick overview of each:

1. Traditional Format: In this format, individual classes of children are organized around specific ages/grades. The students in each class, for the most part, sit, listen, and respond to a teacher "up front." There is some form of lesson review/reinforcement usually delivered in a written way. Perhaps the biggest advantage to this format is that it requires less week-to-week, onsite coordination. Once the classes are established and the teacher and student materials obtained, each teacher and class manage and move forward on their own following the established curriculum and calendar of lessons. This format presents some challenges too. It can be expensive, as it frequently requires more printed lesson materials for staff and children. It necessitates volunteers who have the gifts and skills to effectively prepare and orchestrate the whole morning on their own (teach lessons well, facilitate reinforcement activities, manage students, etc.). It requires more self-contained spaces for each class. Staff may need to be present more Sundays in a row to maintain continuity. It's also the format most like "another day of school."

2. Stations Format: In this format, smaller groups of children, usually organized around age/grade (although they could also be mixed ages/grades) move/rotate through a series of stations at which various parts of the lesson are

presented by different staff who become the "expert" presenter(s) for their station. For example, one station is the lesson presentation itself, another station the discussion of the lesson or a video retelling, another a craft or physical reinforcement activity, another perhaps a song that relates to the lesson. The advantages of this format are that it provides a nice variety of content and exposure to more staff for all the children. It requires less dedicated spaces as you only need as many spaces as the stations offered. It allows students to physically move. If groups would be mixed ages/grades (at least some of the time), younger and older children would have opportunities to grow in their care and encouragement of each other. It also spreads the lesson-teaching duties to more than just one volunteer. There are also some challenges with this format. One would be finding volunteers with the required "expertise" for each station. Another would be effectively tying together all station's content with the main lesson and its truth, seeing as different groups would begin at different stations (unless your enrollment is small enough to have all children start at the lesson presentation station). This format also requires more advanced coordination and planning in order to ensure each station offers meaningful content and supports/advances the main lesson theme. There are also the logistics of the station-to-station movement.

3. Large Group / Small Group Format: In this format, the lesson for the week—using PowerPoint or a similar program—augmented with video, music, and singing is taught by a more "expert" person(s) to all students together (large group). This is followed by individual grade / age-specific classes staying together and moving to reinforcement activities in their assigned classrooms/spaces (small groups). There are advantages to this format. It provides variety and the opportunity for children to move. The large group reinforces a "Sunday school family" culture in that it brings everyone (staff, children, all ages) together. It enables all

children to hear a high-quality main lesson from the same teacher(s) whose Bible knowledge and gifts for teaching all ages, singing, using technology, as well as the time to prepare the lesson, exceed that of others on the staff. Having very qualified staff present the main lesson takes the pressure off other staff who may feel less confident in their abilities and gifts for presenting the lesson accurately and in engaging ways. That the main lesson each week is presented by the "A-Team" frequently enhances volunteer recruiting for small groups as the responsibilities for preparing and presenting these activities are not as daunting. Challenges with the large group / small group format are these: (1) Having a big enough space for the whole Sunday school to gather for a large group. (2) Access to high-quality technology (projector, screen, sound system). (3) Finding qualified staff to develop and effectively deliver the large group lesson to all the children at once. (4) Efficiently transitioning between large and small groups. (5) Developing meaningful and diverse small group activities week to week that reinforce the lesson.

Traditional, stations, large group / small group—three formats that could be used to present a high-quality Sunday school ministry. Each could be offered effectively if the right things are done, curriculum modifications are made, and the best people are in place to make them "winners."

Over my forty-plus-year career, God has blessed me with experience and success using all three formats. In the interest of full disclosure, however, the format I liked being a part of the most was the large group / small group. This format, in my opinion, has the greatest potential for making a high-quality Sunday school where the Word of Life comes to life in upbeat, interactive, fun, and faith-nurturing ways. Permit me to share how I did it in my last church, and remember what I said at the very beginning of this book: "I am no expert!"

In the large group / small group format, all the children in the Sunday school (ages 4K to grade 6), after they were checked into their individual classes, came together in the large group space where kids' Bible songs and music would be playing. After a welcome, a twenty-five- to thirty-minute lesson for the week was presented using PowerPoint (PPT). The PPT was highly visual, colorful, and served as the "roadmap" for the large group session.

The PPT began with a review of what Sunday it was and the singing of our special Sunday school theme song. This usually was followed by another familiar video song we used in a previous lesson(s). Both songs included on-screen words and physical actions. Next, would be a quick review of the previous week's lesson/truth, using a couple of images and or phrases from the previous week to jog memories and to "catch up" children who had missed. Then a "setup" of some kind was used to introduce the idea/truth being covered in the new lesson. A unique image, an on-screen question for pairs to discuss, a video clip, an object I held up that was unique to the lesson, a demonstration, etc. would get the kids' minds "sticky" for the Bible lesson to come.

The setup would segue into the presentation of the lesson showing on-screen Bible passage portions and images that assisted with the lesson telling. Frequently, after this telling, a short video clip, retelling the lesson would be shown. Many times, images from the retelling video would be snipped and inserted into the initial telling of the lesson. This gave the kids some visual "mileposts" to see in the video and assist memory. (Note: If you are using a curriculum with specific, printed Bible story illustrations that are part of the lesson and/or its reinforcement activities, these could be inserted into your Large Group PPT to make helpful memory connections.)

After the lesson telling/retelling and truth review, another video song would be sung that included motions and supported the lesson truth. The PPT-assisted lesson would end with a prayer, a quick "heads-up" about small group activities for the morning, a reminder to come next week, and kids' Bible songs playing in the background as the classes left for small group.

Some curricula, like Group Publishing's "Dig In" series, for example, provide videos for lesson presentation, application, and singing. Other curricula may do the same.

Using technology and PPT is very, very helpful as kids today are highly visual. But be careful to figure out ways to "switch up" your week-to-week lesson presentations, making the presentation (order, parts, content, look, etc.) a little different once in a while to avoid what's called habituation. Habituation is when things become routine, predictable, and repetitive, causing kids to lose interest and tune out. The habituation phenomenon is a concern with any curriculum and format, not just the large group / small group format.

Now a little about finding your own videos to support your weekly lesson. The Internet is a great source for all kinds of biblically accurate, real-life movie clips in addition to animated versions of Bible stories. Make sure, however, to vet for biblical accuracy whatever videos you select. Also make sure your nonvideo telling of the lesson and any video retelling of the lesson are congruent, lest confusion arise in your young believers.

Most of the time, a video the length I wanted was available to convert and download for PPT. Sometimes, I'd need to do some simple editing of the video to get the portion I wanted. I tried to use a combination of real-life and animated videos representing real life so kids would get a good variety, yet also understand that the Bible is not fake, like a cartoon. While some would protest that animated versions of Bible lessons make the Bible less serious and should not be used, I found that they can be very helpful for getting children to see the lesson details and truth.

Some animated videos are very kid-friendly, of high interest, tell the story accurately, and really assist the children in remembering the lesson. I stayed away from animated videos of Bible stories, however, that included goofy, silly, or anachronistic stuff like the robot guy that goes along on Bible adventures in the *Superbook* series. My overall philosophy for using videos was to select ones that presented the Bible lesson accurately, in believable ways, but also in a variety of ways week over week.

Below are some sources for good downloadable animated videos about familiar Bible stories:

- God's Story
- Stories of the Bible—Saddleback Kids
- Slapstick Theater—Saddleback Kids
- The Beginners Bible
- Bible Stories for Kids
- Kids Play and Learn—You Version
- The Story for Teens
- Sharefaith Kids
- Bible Tales for Kids

For videos showing real humans / real-life versions of Bible lesson segments, the search is a little more work. "The Jesus Film"[46] and "The Life of Jesus"[47] are good sources. You could also Google what you needed, for example, "Moses and the Burning Bush" or "David and Goliath."

The "Dig In" curriculum produced by Group Publishing Inc. includes lesson-telling videos, lesson application videos—showing how the lesson truth would be applied in real life—and correlated song videos. Many video songs can also be found by Googling "songs for Sunday school on Vimeo," for example. The curriculum you use may also have great video suggestions. With all videos, you'll want to watch them in their entirety, to familiarize yourself with them and also ensure they are biblically correct and appropriate for your audience.

The large group / small group format assumes all levels of students have the same Bible lesson each week. If you are using a different format, say individual classes in their own rooms or a station-to-station format, using videos is still a great way to present or reinforce the Bible lesson for the week.

For the small group portion of the lesson, students return in their assigned groups to their individual classes. The adult/teen leaders and students quickly review/retell what the large group lesson was about and do the reinforcement activities. With every reinforcement activity, connections are made to the lesson and its theme/truth. Reinforcement activities could include more discussion/application questions in smaller subgroups, a craft, a more physical/movement activity, an object lesson, role-playing, an experiment of some kind, a game, and a closing wrap-up summary and prayer.

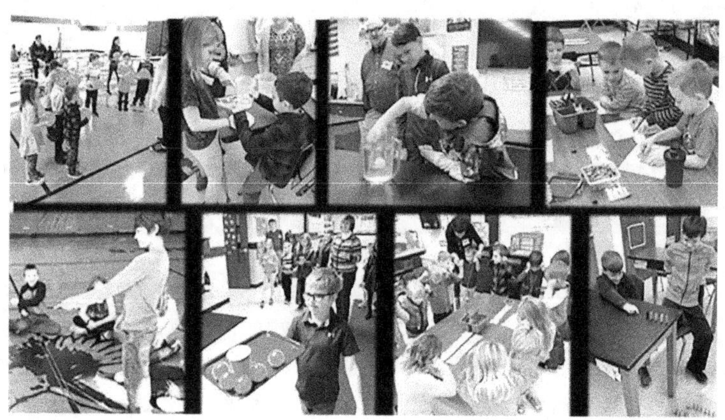

Some curricula, like Group Inc.'s "Dig In" provide a buffet of reinforcement things to do with their lessons. Other curricula might also. If not, you can do some online research and/or make up your own small group reinforcement activities. But these activities should be determined well in advance of the lesson they accompany so that materials can be obtained and staff can be prepared.

Googling "interactive reinforcement activities for Sunday school" provides numerous results, but you'll need to vet them all also. Here, too, it is good to have a variety of small group activities week to week and enough of them each week to fill the twenty-five- to thirty-minute small group time.

Nine-year-old Joey was asked by his mother what he had learned in Sunday school. "Well, Mom, our teacher told us how God sent Moses behind enemy lines on a rescue mission to lead the Israelites out of Egypt. When he got to the Red Sea, he had his army build a pontoon bridge, and all the people walked across safely. Then he radioed headquarters for reinforcements. They sent bombers to blow up the bridge, and all the Israelites were saved."

"Now, Joey, is that really what your teacher taught you?" his mother asked.

"Well, no, Mom. But if I told it the way the teacher did, you'd never believe it!"

There's no joking with Joey. The Bible is filled with incredible stories of God working his will in unbelievable ways. Being able to share these stories is what makes Sunday school teaching so wonderful and fun. Whatever Joey's Sunday school teacher did and however she presented the miraculous details of the lesson left an impression on him.

Did the teacher raise and lower the pitch of her voice? Did she whisper and shout? Did she move around the room and lift her arms like Moses might have? Did she pass around a long staff like the one God helped Moses turn into a snake? Did she share pictures of frogs, lice, flies, hail, and locusts? Did she have the kids shout out, "Let my people go!" Did she show video clips from Cecil B. DeMille's *The Ten Commandments* or other movies?

How we present the Sunday school lessons to the children we are privileged to serve in Christ's name is huge. We dare never change the content or become a roadblock. We for sure need to be great conduits through which the Holy Spirit can work as we accommodate and engage their God-given learning styles. The format we use—the structure/framework we follow—is key too. Determining the best format for your setting is part of the fun as well.

5. Offer Top-Notch Training

A man was delivering penguins to the zoo when his van broke down on the highway. A fellow stopped to see if he could be of assistance. "Oh, I'm in some real trouble here," said the first man. "I've got to take these penguins to the zoo today, and now I'm not sure I'll get there."

The helpful fellow volunteered to put the penguins in the back of his car and take them to the zoo. The man with car trouble gratefully accepted this offer and promised to get to the zoo as soon as possible.

A little later, the man was on the road again and went immediately to the zoo. He looked everywhere but did not see the helpful fellow or any of the penguins. In a panic, he drove back into town. Just as he was wondering what in the world to do next, he saw the volunteer walking across the street with all the penguins waddling along behind him.

He ran up and said, "What are you doing here? I thought you were going to take the penguins to the zoo!"

The volunteer replied, "I did, and we had such a good time there, we decided to come into town for ice cream."

Moral of the story: when working with volunteers, clear instructions and good training is always necessary.

Clear instructions and good training. In part 2 of this book, we talked about Sunday school being *the* opportunity for many children to learn about Jesus. In that section was this quote from Alan Loy McGinnis: "People do not like being lethargic and bored. They will welcome the manager who can teach them to enjoy their work, or the teacher who will impart to them a love of learning that causes the school day to go swiftly." This quote, with its phrases "teach them to enjoy" and "impart to them," speaks to the training we give those volunteering in our Sunday school ministries.

If we are running a quality Sunday school, what should those volunteering or interested in volunteering be able to expect training-wise from those leading the effort. The following list explores the expectations.

What Should the Sunday School Staff Expect?

1. A positive and clear articulation of the Sunday school's mission/vision.

Can staff members (present and potential) see what the point and purpose of Sunday school is? Can they grasp the "white hot why" for its existence? Do they clearly see how Sunday school fits into the total ministry of the congregation? Unless the staff members know this, there is no way they can plug in totally. Every credible and successful organization, has a mission statement that directs its efforts and focuses its activity. The fact that the mission statement is written down tells everyone that the program is important. Someone took the time to think things through and get on paper what the purpose and point really are. Everyone can, therefore, be "on the same page." That the mission statement is positive, communicates an emotion and feeling about Sunday school ministry. If people cannot identify and connect emotionally with the effort, they will not remain for long.

Finally, everyone wants to be connected to a winner. A mission statement that clearly expresses the joy we have in serving Jesus will provide the best reason for wanting to be a part of the Sunday school team. "Jesus Christ has won the victory! Praise God we're winners in him!"

2. A clear description/understanding (preferably in writing) of what their job and commitment will be.

Every ministry program wants committed people involved in it. But the committed people we want as Sunday school teachers are also committed in every other aspect of their lives. Research indicates that everyone wants to be a part of something meaningful, but frequently people cannot be involved in the way they are being asked. Committed people do not have the time to wonder what the job is about and how much time and effort it will take. They want to know and need to know these details up front: What will I be doing? When will it happen? How long will it take? What do I use? How long do you expect me to do it? Who else is helping?

Then they can ponder the position, pray about it, and make an intelligent decision that will truly help the ministry and be good for them as disciples of Jesus. People don't have time or desire to spin their wheels, figuring everything out as they go. Wheel spinning creates friction and heat, and people who spend too much time spinning their wheels eventually (like tires) burn out.

A Sunday school program that cannot show prospective teachers what their job will be, communicates that it is disorganized, lacks clear direction, and doesn't really care about the people involved. Letting potential volunteers know up front what the job is all about will make it possible for them to commit with confidence…theirs and yours.

3. A complete orientation regarding the position, work, team
   members, meetings, chain of command, responsibilities, budget,
   curriculum, etc.

In today's human resources parlance, it's called onboarding. Onboarding refers to the processes in which new hires are integrated into the organization. It includes activities that allow new employees to complete an initial new-hire orientation process, as well as learn about the organization and its structure, culture, vision, mission, and values.

An onboarding orientation is a good idea for Sunday school staff too. This orientation need not be long, but it does need to be thorough. The more volunteers know up front, the better they will be able to evaluate their level of involvement. Good orientation says, "Great leadership." If you are the Sunday school leader and can't present this information in a clear, complete, and congenial way, you've got some work to do.

Your Sunday school onboarding should especially include the calendar of lessons and any special activities for the year, like when kids sing in church, when staff meetings will be, etc. Planning for a whole year in advance is commonplace today. In fact, many organizations plan even further out than that. While things do change and adjustments need to be made, planning out the whole Sunday school year accomplishes several good things.

First, it says, "We are organized and are thinking ahead." It tells teachers and parents that the Sunday school ministry leaders have done their homework and that the program is not flying by the seat of its evangelical pants. People need to see the whole picture if they are going to construct a proper understanding of what's going on. If the Sunday school is in a congregation that also operates a Christian elementary school, the advanced planning can head off unnecessary and aggravating duplications and conflicts.

Second, knowing the schedule in advance frees the teachers to concentrate on the agreed upon lessons rather than spend time wondering what would be good to present each week. A complete calendar of lessons enables a teacher to determine their availability to teach week to week and more importantly, think ahead about applications, demonstrations, activities, and objects that will enhance their lesson for the students.

4. A solid promise that program meetings will be regular, upbeat, organized, meaningful, and reasonable.

Every quality effort involving people needs to have some team together time. Most people say they hate meetings, but it's probably not because of the need to meet. It's probably because the meeting was a pointless pain.

My brother, also in church work, once wrote an article for a denominational magazine. The article was titled "We've Got to Stop Meeting Like This!" and talked about the high number of "church meetings" that take place. One funny line from the article said something like this: "One good thing about all these meetings is that when Jesus returns, I'll probably be at church." Sunday school staff meetings should not be pointless or painful. They should be…

- *Regular.* Regular staff meetings communicate that the ministry is vital and that there is an organized plan to it all.

Hit-and-miss staff meetings produce come-and-go teachers. Whether monthly, quarterly, or some other known and steady duration, meetings should happen to demonstrate seriousness. Regular meetings are needed to discuss items, issues, and information vital to the ministry's success. Meetings that are regularly scheduled are a courteous and professional way to acknowledge that committed, busy people need to plan. Regular meetings can also help to establish a great Sunday school team culture.

- *Upbeat.* Staff meetings need to be upbeat because our God can raise people from the dead! We are sooooo happy about what Jesus has done for us, aren't we? Also, upbeat meetings are a lot more fun to attend, and if I have fun at the meeting, I'll come back again. Did I mention that "Jesus Christ has won the victory"? Play some music. Have some snacks. Smile and laugh. Enjoy each other and what you are doing together in Christ's name. I bet Jesus and his disciples had all kinds of good times together.

- *Organized.* When my youngest daughter, Lindsay, was in kindergarten, she went to class one day and along with her classmates followed all the pre-bell procedures for being ready for class. When the bell rang, the teacher was still at her desk, fumbling with papers, pencils, and books. My daughter, not quite grasping the gravity of the moment, yelled out, "At least some of us are organized today!" That resulted in a memorable parent-teacher meeting for sure. But an important point was made. If a five-year-old can deduce disorganization, imagine what a teen or adult can think. Well-organized meetings show that Sunday school is a priority and that the Sunday school leaders have taken the time needed to make it the best. Time and attention spans are too short to be wasted at meetings that drag along in a "go nowhere, do nothing" mode. The Sunday school leader needs to have his/her team meeting ducks in a row. While organization may not be your gift, you can learn the skills. Remember, you are the "lengthened shadow," establishing a winning culture with others whose time, like yours, is very precious. Hand out a written agenda, provide the needed ancillary materials, and start and end on time. Run the meeting in such a manner that at the end, your team members are saying to each other, "We're done already?" rather than singing, "Praise God from Whom all blessings flow."

- *Meaningful.* Teachers grow who are being fed with the Word and with helpful teaching strategies and approaches at meaningful meetings. And you know what else? Their teaching gets better, their students come more often, and parents are more supportive. If you want the Sunday school and its volunteers to grow in positive ways, what's covered at the meeting must contribute to this meaningfulness. Make things fun, but stick to the point. Follow an agenda that includes a welcome and team-sharing/check-in (five minutes); opening devotion/Bible study, song, and prayer (twenty minutes); relevant staff development topic to make themselves and the ministry better—improving lesson review, effective use of video, accommodating learning styles, etc. (twenty minutes); program "nuts and bolts"—upcoming lessons, attendance data/concerns, supplies needs, emergency procedures, etc. (five minutes); students/families needing prayers and support (five minutes); and questions and closing benediction/song (five minutes). You want people to feel, "This was worth the time."

- *Reasonable.* The agenda components and timeframes in the previous section are suggestions, but shooting to be done in sixty to seventy-five minutes will make your volunteers move up your name on their Christmas shopping list. Everyone is busy these days, and that's not always sinful. It's just life and blessings from God. Your staff members have their own lives and families. The church and its activities should not be another thing that pulls these families apart.

When I taught Sunday school in high school, the superintendent had staff meetings every week. I look back at that now and wonder how in the world we did it. Today, depending on your curriculum and your staff's experience, you may be able to meet together twice a month, monthly, quarterly, or even just a couple times a year. Meeting less frequently may mean a bit longer meeting, but that could be a welcome trade-off if it helps bring excellence to what you do and enhances the joy of serving.

5. Confidence that everything they need to do
   the job will be there when they need it.

The most significant part of teaching is preparation, and a good Sunday school will encourage its staff members to prepare well in advance. But stressing advanced preparation is pointless if the needed materials are not there. Waiting for things can frustrate even the most dedicated and patient teacher. Retaining staff and recruiting new staff members is enhanced greatly when teachers can feel confident about getting the needed resources well in advance. Nothing crumbles the commitment of a volunteer more than not having the tools they need to do the job you talked them into taking. Teacher's books, student books, Bibles, paper, pencils, glue, scissors, paper towels, activities materials, working technology, whatever is required for them to do their Sunday school job needs to be available.

One church I am aware of had a special supplies cart for each class level. Always on the cart were the weekly needed items (pencils, markers, scissors, glue, paper towels, wet wipes, etc.). Any new materials/supplies for a lesson were added to the cart each week by staff assigned to manage the lesson supplies. The class teacher/aide simply got the right cart and rolled it to class. Boy, did that make things easier for everyone!

Sunday school teachers are some of the most gifted and dedicated people around. They are also some of the most generous, voluntarily contributing from their own financial resources to support the Sunday school ministry. But should they have to? Could the fact that, in some settings, there is an expectation that the Sunday school teacher will need to "kick in" for his/her class materials and supplies be a reason to not get involved? While volunteers might be hyper-generous, they should not be expected to buy and "donate" the items needed for their class. If teachers might need to get some of the things they need/want for their lessons, then a budget should allow for their reimbursement up to a reasonable limit. Being able to say during the onboarding meeting, "The church will provide everything you'll need for class as well as a $50 budget (for example) per class, just in case," will be very reassuring to the volunteer. Losing a good volunteer because they cannot afford to or don't have the time to buy church ministry materials would be very sad.

6. A sure trust that the rest of the team is just that:
   the rest of the team.

The cartoon below says it all. Teamwork makes the dream work. Coming together is a beginning. Keeping together is progress. Working together is success. It's even more important in a Sunday school.

Satan wants to rip things apart. He wants the Jesus stuff stopped. He gleefully pats himself on the back when the unspoken motto of a church ministry is, "We're all in this...alone."

A quality Sunday school ministry has a staff that knows and trusts its members share the same faith, focus, and feelings about what they are doing. A quality Sunday school ministry has a staff that knows teamwork is...

- The fulfillment of God's design.
  "Now to each one the manifestation of the Spirit is given for the common good... The body is a unit, though it is made up of many parts; and though all its parts are many, they form one body. So it is with Christ. For we were all baptized by one Spirit into one body—whether Jews or Greeks, slave or free—and we were all given the one Spirit to drink. Now the body is not made up of one part but of many...God has arranged the parts in the body, every one of them, just as he wanted them to be... If they were all one part, where would the body be?... [T]hose parts of the body that seem to be weaker are indispensable, and the parts that we think are less honorable we treat with special honor... But God has combined the members of the body... so that there should be no division in the body, but that its parts should have equal concern for each other... Now you are the body of Christ, and each one of you is a part of it" (1 Corinthians 12 NIV).

- An opportunity for individual and collective growth.
  "As iron sharpens iron, so one man sharpens another" (Proverbs 27:17).

- A support that leads to better results.
  "Two are better than one, because they have a good return for their work: If one falls down, his friend can help him up. But pity the man who falls and has no one to help him up!" (Ecclesiastes 4:9–10).

- A test of the sincerity of our love and service.
  "Above all, love each other deeply, because love covers over a multitude of sins. Offer hospitality to one another without grumbling. Each one should use whatever gift he has received to serve others, faithfully administering God's grace in its various forms" (1 Peter 4:8–10).

A Sunday school staff can be a wonderful, real-world example of the body of Christ in action (Romans 12, 1 Corinthians 12). And there is nothing more wonderful for students and parents to see than a Sunday school staff that openly "one-anothers" each other like so many passages in Scripture say. A Sunday school staff that lovingly works as a team, nurturing and supporting each other's spiritual and pedagogical growth, also models what it means to be a family of believers.

7. The Sunday school leader's appreciation as well as the appreciation of the congregation and its leaders.

I am sure that if you asked Sunday school teachers, "What payment do you receive for teaching Sunday school?" you would get answers like these: "The smiles of my students' faces as they learn about Jesus." "The joy of knowing that God is using me to share the Good News with others." "The self-satisfaction of using my time and talents to serve my Savior."

Until Sunday school staff positions become paid ones, that's the kind of compensation that can be expected. For sure, the "compensations" mentioned by teachers are wonderful, but could something more be given? I think so, and it could simply be the private and public thanks of the congregation's leadership.

Do what the late Lorene Nelson taught. Lorene was my mom. If she was present and someone gave me a gift, paid me a compliment, or did anything remotely nice for me, she'd look in my direction and ask, "What do you say?" It was wonderful training. Sometimes, however, Lorene was quicker than required.

I remember a couple of times after someone had done or said something nice to me in the presence of my mother, with my lips already twittering and my voice box vibrating, ready to express my thanks, Lorene would ask, "What do you say?" One such time, I lost it. I said, "Geeeeeeeeeezzz, Mom, can you give a guy a chance?"

Again, what my mom did was wonderful training. She knew it was important for the receiver of good things to express appreciation. She also wisely knew that the giver of good things benefitted from the "thank yous" too.

I've never met a person whose motivation for joining a volunteer effort was because of the praise and adoration they'd get for doing it. In fact, most volunteers say they don't want any recognition or praise. Our own human nature, research done on volunteerism, and the Lorene Nelson's in the world reveal, however, that tangible recognition and appreciation for things done brings joy and a sense of satisfaction and fulfillment.

Volunteer appreciation is also a vital part of retention and recruitment. Volunteers who feel noticed and appreciated are much more likely not only to keep at it but also to spread the word that what they are doing is worth being a part of. Prioritizing volunteer appreciation is important for a Sunday school ministry's long-term success.

Research done by the Gallup Organization (Princeton, New Jersey) in 2001 revealed twelve factors that help congregation members stay actively engaged in their churches. The factors are noted below as if they were spoken by the member him/herself. Note numbers 4–6:

1. As a member of my congregation, I know what is expected of me.
2. In my congregation, my spiritual needs are met.
3. In my congregation, I regularly have the opportunity to do what I do best.
4. In the last month, I have received recognition or praise from someone in my congregation.

5. The spiritual leaders in my congregation seem to care about me as a person.
6. There is someone in my congregation who encourages my spiritual development.
7. As a member of my congregation, my opinions seem to count.
8. The mission or purpose of my congregation makes me feel my participation is important.
9. The other members of my congregation are committed to spiritual growth.
10. Aside from family members, I have a best friend in my congregation.
11. In the last six months, someone in my congregation has talked to me about the progress of my spiritual growth.
12. In my congregation, I have opportunities to learn and grow.

Receiving a card, note, text, email, or phone call from the pastor, congregation chairman, church council, or Christian education board members can go a long way toward helping volunteer staff members feel they are appreciated and needed. It can help them to know that they do not serve in a vacuum but rather are part of the congregation's total mission and ministry. It can stress the team and "one-anothering" concepts at an even higher level.

Showing appreciation in more public ways can also help the entire congregation to recognize its responsibility to encourage, pray for, and financially support the Sunday school ministry and its staff.

I have heard it said that Christian duty means we serve God and others and should not expect to be thanked for doing what we are supposed to do. While it is true that Christians are to serve God and others, how wonderful it is when Christian duty is nurtured and encouraged with Christian love. Showing more love, support, and appreciation for Sunday school staff members may just result in happier teachers, who do their jobs even better, reflect their joy in Jesus even more, and remain Sunday school teachers for a long, long time.

A quality Sunday school ministry needs to offer its volunteers top-notch onboarding and training. Volunteers usually have expectations when it comes to their involvement. They are helped tremendously when they receive,

- A positive and clear articulation of the Sunday school's mission/vision.
- A clear description/understanding (preferably in writing) of what their job and commitment will be.
- A complete orientation regarding the position, work, team members, meetings, chain of command, responsibilities, budget, curriculum, etc.
- A solid promise that program meetings will be regular, upbeat, organized, meaningful, and reasonable.
- Confidence that everything they need to do the job will be there when they need it.
- A sure trust that the rest of the team is just that: the rest of the team.
- The Sunday school leader's appreciation as well as the appreciation of the congregation and its leaders.

Is providing the above impossible? No. Is it involved? A little. Is it beneficial? *Absotively posilutely!*

How do we make a quality Sunday school happen? Adjust your attitude. Leverage good leadership. Use the correct curriculum. Favor a winning format. Offer top-notch training.

Praying for and relentlessly working on all of these, year after year, in your Sunday school will "raise the bar" in dramatic ways. It will help you become a winning Sunday school ministry that serves Jesus and his children well.

Part 6

How Do We Get and Keep the Winning Sunday School Team?

Ever hear this one: "The ark was built by volunteers; the Titanic was built by professionals"? Ask any director of a nonprofit or pastor at a church about volunteers, and you'll probably be told they are mighty important. Their effort makes such a positive and lasting impact. They enable the organization to exist and fulfill its mission.

One of the big questions for any organization relying heavily on volunteers is, "How do we get and keep them?" When it comes to running a high-quality Sunday school, finding and keeping volunteers is not as hard as we think.

In part 5, this statement was made: "People don't have time or desire to spin their wheels, figuring everything out as they go. Wheel spinning creates friction and heat, and people who spend too much time spinning their wheels eventually (like tires) burn out." This statement was also noted: "Volunteers who feel noticed and appreciated are much more likely not only to keep at it but also to spread the word that what they are doing is worth being a part of." In part 3, this simple but profound statement was given: "People do not like being lethargic and bored. They will welcome the manager who can teach them to enjoy their work… Everyone wants to be connected to a winner." In those three statements lie a simple "formula" for getting and keeping volunteers.

At the outset of this book, I said this about myself: "I'm not comfortable being called an expert, but I have experienced and studied a lot on the subject. I know stuff. You'll have to decide how much of my stuff becomes your stuff." On the subject of getting and keeping Sunday school volunteers, here's the stuff I have learned and know for a fact.

1. If people trust that the congregation truly loves its children and their families as well as children and families in the community like Jesus does, they will be more interested in stepping up and staying involved.
2. If people grasp that Sunday school is an integral part of the congregation's ministry to save and serve souls for all eternity, they will be more interested in stepping up and staying involved.
3. If people have total confidence in the ability, dedication, support, and love of the Sunday school leader(s), they will be more interested in stepping up and staying involved.
4. If people see that the Sunday school ministry is an organized, positive, fun, meaningful, and "winning" effort, they will be more interested in stepping up and staying involved.
5. If people learn there are others excited about and happily involved in the Sunday school ministry, they will be more interested in stepping up and staying involved.
6. If people hear that Sunday school students and families really love the ministry and are growing in faith because of it, they will be more interested in stepping up and staying involved.
7. If people can easily learn as much as they can about the Sunday school ministry *before* they make any kind of commitment, they will be more interested in stepping up and staying involved.
8. If people are presented with specific and reasonable involvement parameters (for example, we need two helpers, adult or teen, to assist with third- to fourth-grade small groups,

two Sundays a month for one hour, 9:00–10:00 a.m., September to December), they will be more interested in stepping up and staying involved.

9. If people sense that their time and effort will be appreciated and recognized by the Sunday school leader, the elected church leaders, and the broader Sunday school and church family, they will be more interested in stepping up and staying involved.

10. If people, especially ones you know have the gifts you are looking for, can receive a personal invitation to meet and then have a highly informative, compelling, but low-pressure face-to-face sit down to chat about the Sunday school ministry and their potential partnership in it, they will be more interested in stepping up and staying involved.

More pie in the sky? No. The above is not a small list, but it's certainly not an impossible one. The wonderful reality is that the more successful and excellent your Sunday school becomes, the easier it is to accomplish what's on the list. If done seriously and well, you may experience what I did: people asking to become part of the Sunday school ministry before you started recruiting them. Yup, that actually happened, several times.

Part 7

Final Encouragements

Little Johnny and his family were having Sunday dinner at his grandmother's house. Everyone was seated around the table as the food was being served. When Little Johnny received his plate, he started eating right away.

"Johnny! Please wait until we say our prayer," said his mother.

"I don't need to," the boy replied.

"Of course, you do," his mother insisted. "We always say a prayer before eating at our house."

"That's at our house," Johnny explained. "But this is Grandma's house, and she knows how to cook!"

Uninhibited and insightful, Johnny knows what he knows. When it comes to Sunday school, kids and parents know what they know too. They can see if a Sunday school ministry is professional, organized, and current. They can tell if its leaders, staff, and volunteers are qualified and capable. They can sense how serious the congregation is about the Sunday school's mission, ministry, and membership.

I love Sunday school! Of all the things I was responsible for and did over forty-plus years of ministry (teacher, principal, dean of students, youth and family minister, discipleship director, national office executive), I have to say being involved with Sunday schools was the favorite.

As was noted in the introduction, this book was written because I believe in Sunday schools. They are the Christian education ministry impacting the most children across the country, maybe even the world. I went to them. I taught in them. I supervised them. I championed them. I also saw the spiritual, mental, physical, and emotional good the Holy Spirit works through this timeless form of ministry. I want Sunday schools to succeed at the highest levels and continue to have the most optimum impact. I want all Sunday schools to be *winners*! I believe they absolutely can.

Sunday schools, because they are an effort connected to God's Word, have God's promises and providence behind them. God does the real work. God's divine will is always done. God's Word always accomplishes its purpose. What God ordains is always good.

Sunday schools are also a human effort, touched by sinners and tainted by sin's impact on the world. We don't mean to, but sometimes we put roadblocks in the Holy Spirit's way. Our purpose, our priorities, our planning, and our preparation get befuddled.

Sometimes our prayers about Sunday school are also a problem. We may ask, "Dear Heavenly Father, please bless what we're doing," rather than, "Dear Heavenly Father, please help us see and do what you will bless." There is a big difference. While all Sunday schools sharing the good news of Jesus have God's blessing on them, some seem to have God's blessings more than others. This book is trying to express that there are good reasons for this.

I don't believe anything written to this point is ridiculous or radical. I've prayed that my "pen" produces clear and nonheretical thoughts. Some ideas may be new. Some may move you to think, reflect, evaluate, and ponder like never before. Some may challenge assumptions you've had and practices you've maintained. Some might even make you a little uncomfortable.

I have advanced degrees in education and leadership. I've had to "read" a lot of books over the years in order to get those degrees. I put "read" in quotes because I must admit that a lot of what these books covered I can't remember. But I can tell you there were always a few valuable nuggets taken from each one.

My prayer is that you have discovered some valuable nuggets in these pages and will use them to raise the bar and pursue "winning" improvement in your Sunday school. God's richest blessings on your effort.

Jesus Christ has won the victory; praise God we're winners in him!

Part 8

Questions for Team Discussion

Part 1: Who Am I / Who Are You? (See pages 1-4)

1. Why are you reading this book?
2. What do you feel about the new names given to "Sunday school" ministries?
3. Do Cynthia Tobias's words make sense to you? Explain.
4. How much of "an oasis" is your current Sunday school for the kids participating in it?
5. If you teach/help with Sunday school, what would you do to make things better?

Part 2: What Do You See? (See pages 5-6)

1. Be honest. Which of the two colorful picture explanations (good news / bad news) would describe your current Sunday school ministry? Explain.
2. What are some "beautiful/wonderful things" in your Sunday school?
3. What are some things that could use a "do-over"?
4. In this part you read, "Sunday school advancement and success in any Christian church is God's doing, not ours. We dare not take the credit for God's work," Where do you see God's work in your Sunday school?

5. You also read, "We...must not become a roadblock for the Holy Spirit." What might this roadblock look like?

Part 3: Why Do We Care About Sunday School? (See pages 7-22)

1. Why do *you* care about Sunday school? Do you feel your congregation shares your care?
2. In the Mark 10:13–16 incident (endnote 13), why might the disciples have wanted children to "beat it" and go away? Why did Jesus want the children to stay?
3. How might a poor Sunday school ministry unintentionally/subconsciously communicate to kids (and their parents) a "beat it / go away" vibe?
4. Do the four reasons for caring about Sunday school make sense to you? Explain. Could you add any more?
5. Can you share any examples from your own Sunday school experience (if applicable) to support any of the four reasons for caring about Sunday school, given in this part?

Part 4: What Do We Want Sunday School to Be? (See pages 23-34)

1. Share any reactions you had to the, "I know the answer is Jesus...but it sure sounds like a squirrel to me!" story in this part?
2. Do you feel the distinction between Sunday school as a place to "learn about Jesus" versus "experience Jesus" is a legitimate one? Explain.
3. What have you been taught concerning the Proverbs 22:6 passage? How does Jody Capehart's additional way of looking at it strike you?
4. Share anything about the three basic learning styles/modalities that was an "Aha!" to you? Why is it important to keep learning styles/modalities in our minds as we prepare and present Sunday school lessons?
5. Agree/Disagree: Modeling and maintaining an unconditional love Sunday school ministry can only be done if

those running the Sunday school are personally growing in their own knowledge and appreciation of the unconditional love shown them in Jesus.

Part 5: How Do We Make a Quality Sunday School Happen? (See pages 35-64)

1. React. Sunday school staff members having a "winning" attitude about Jesus means the Sunday school itself will be viewed as a "winning" ministry in the eyes of its students and families.
2. This might be a tough question, but it's a vital one to consider: What kind of "lengthened shadow" is your current Sunday school leadership casting on the Sunday school ministry?
3. What components in your current Sunday school curriculum do you appreciate? What, if added, would make it better?
4. How would you define the "format" used in your Sunday school? Is it working well? Explain. Could a large group / small group format make a positive difference if implemented? Explain.
5. Which of the seven expectations in the "Offer Top-Notch Training" section resonated with you the most? Explain.

Part 6: How Do We Get and Keep a Winning Sunday School Team? (See pages 65-67)

1. What's your opinion on the value of volunteers?
2. If applicable, how did you become part of your Sunday school's ministry?
3. What does Sunday school volunteer recruitment look like in your congregation?
4. Which of the ten "recruiting" statements made sense to you? Explain.
5. Evaluate: the more successful and excellent your Sunday school becomes, the easier it is to find volunteers for it.

Endnotes

1   Barna Research Releases in Faith & Christianity (2005, July 11). "Sunday School is Changing in Under-the-Radar but Significant Ways." https://www. barna.com/research/sunday-school-is-changing-in-under-the-radar-but-significant-ways.

2   This data was provided via email (Thu, Nov 17, 2022, 10:03 a.m.) from D. Scott Kostencki, Director of Rosters, Statistics and Research Services, Lutheran Church Missouri Synod International Center, 1333 South Kirkwood Road, Kirkwood, Missouri.

3   Commission on Discipleship Report. *Wisconsin Evangelical Lutheran Synod 2021 Book of Reports and Memorials*, 35.

4   Childstats Forum on Child and Family Statistics. "POP1 Child population: Number of children (in millions) ages 0–17 in the United States by age, 1950–2021 and projected 2022–2050." https://www.childstats.gov/americaschildren/tables/pop1.asp.

5   The first sentence in the first chapter titled "Loomings" in *Moby Dick* by Herman Melville begins with the words, "Call me Ishmael."

6   Dr. Joel Nelson served in these 7 positions/calls: grades 7–8 teacher and school principal (St. Andrew-Chicago, IL), grades 1–8 teacher and school principal (Our Redeemer-Santa Barbara, CA), Youth and Family Minister (St. Paul's-Muskego, WI), National Associate Director for Parish Schools (Wisconsin Evangelical Lutheran Synod-Milwaukee, WI), National Executive Director of Youth Discipleship (Wisconsin Evangelical Lutheran Synod-Milwaukee, WI), Principal and Dean of Students (Garden Homes-Milwaukee, WI), Director of Discipleship (St. Paul's-Muskego, WI).

7   Dr. Joel Nelson has a BS in education from Martin Luther College–New Ulm, MN; an MS in education/family studies from Concordia University-Mequon, WI, and an EdD in leadership for the advancement of learning and service from Cardinal Stritch University-Milwaukee, WI.

8   Cynthia Ulrich Tobias is the founder, manager, and CEO of Apple St. LLC (Applied Learning Styles) and president of Learning Styles Unlimited Inc. She coordinates the Apple St. education and commerce programs and administers various learning styles projects throughout North America and internationally. Her quote is from an interview Dr. Joel Nelson did with her at the 2001, Wis-

consin Evangelical Lutheran Synod National Education Conference at Martin Luther College in New Ulm, MN.

9   Isaiah 55:11 (NIV): "…so is my word that goes out from my mouth: It will not return to me empty, but will accomplish what I desire and achieve the purpose for which I sent it."

10   On page 38 of *Principles and Methods of Christian Education* (1990), Wisconsin Evangelical Lutheran Synod (WELS) pastor and Wisconsin Lutheran Seminary professor David Kuske wrote, "The objective of the Christian teacher…is not to improve the work of the Holy Spirit or to make the Word of God more powerful. Instead, the objective is a negative one: to avoid any blunders by which we put roadblocks in the way of the Holy Spirit or the power of the Word." Kuske's comments mesh with 1 Thessalonians 5:19 (NIV), "Do not put out the Spirit's fire," and 1 Corinthians 10:32a (NIV), "Do not cause anyone to stumble."

11   Wikipedia entry, W. C. Fields (2022, August 15). https://en.wikipedia.org/wiki/W._C._Fields.

12   Google "W. C. Field's hates children," and watch YouTube videos containing this quote.

13   Mark 10:13–16 (NIV): "People were bringing little children to Jesus for him to place his hands on them, but the disciples rebuked them. When Jesus saw this, he was indignant. He said to them, 'Let the little children come to me, and do not hinder them, for the kingdom of God belongs to such as these. Truly I tell you, anyone who will not receive the kingdom of God like a little child will never enter it.' And he took the children in his arms, placed his hands on them and blessed them."

14   Matthew 28:16–20 (NIV): "Then the eleven disciples went to Galilee, to the mountain where Jesus had told them to go. When they saw him, they worshiped him; but some doubted. Then Jesus came to them and said, 'All authority in heaven and on earth has been given to me. Therefore, go and make disciples of all nations, baptizing them in the name of the Father and of the Son and of the Holy Spirit, and teaching them to obey everything I have commanded you. And surely I am with you always, to the very end of the age.'"

15   The David P. Kuske edition of *Luther's Catechism* (Northwestern Publishing House, Milwaukee, WI, 1984) says this: Q 269: What Does Jesus' command to baptize "all nations" mean? A: Jesus' command to baptize "all nations" means we are to baptize all who request baptism for themselves and for their children. Q 271: Why do we baptize children? A: We baptize children because a) they are included in Christ's words "all nations," b) they are sinful by nature and must be born again in order to be saved, and c) they too can believe.

16   Barna, G. *Ministry Currents*, October–December, 1991, 9.

17   Benson, P., and Eklin, C. "Effective Christian Education: A National Study of Protestant Congregations." Summary Report. Minneapolis: Search Institute, 1990, 58.

18 This quote is from author Thom Schultz's interview with a Sunday school student recorded in *Why Nobody Learns Much of Anything at Church and How to Fix It*, Group Publishing, 1993, 9.

19 McGinnis, A. L. *Bringing Out the Best in People*, Augsburg Publishing House, Minneapolis, 1985, 19.

20 First Corinthians 10:31 (NIV): "So whether you eat or drink or whatever you do, do it all for the glory of God."

21 First Corinthians 14:40 (NIV): "But everything should be done in a fitting and orderly way."

22 Bible Truth Publishers. *Moody Stories*. https://bibletruthpublishers.com/moodys-stories/dwight-l-moody/lbd41523.

23 BrainyQuote.com. "Martin Luther King Jr. Quotes." https://www.brainyquote.com/ quotes/martin_luther_king_jr_137105.

24 BrainyQuote.com. "Rick Warren Quotes." https://www.brainyquote.com/ quotes/ rick_warren_395868.

25 First Peter 4:10–11 (NIV): "Each of you should use whatever gift you have received to serve others, as faithful stewards of God's grace in its various forms. If anyone speaks, they should do so as one who speaks the very words of God. If anyone serves, they should do so with the strength God provides, so that in all things God may be praised through Jesus Christ. To him be the glory and the power for ever and ever. Amen." Romans 12:6–8 (NIV): "We have different gifts, according to the grace given to each of us. If your gift is prophesying, then prophesy in accordance with your faith; if it is serving, then serve; if it is teaching, then teach; if it is to encourage, then give encouragement; if it is giving, then give generously; if it is to lead, do it diligently; if it is to show mercy, do it cheerfully."

26 Proverbs 11:25 (NIV): "A generous person will prosper; whoever refreshes others will be refreshed." Luke 6:38 (NIV): "Give, and it will be given to you. A good measure, pressed down, shaken together and running over, will be poured into your lap. For with the measure you use, it will be measured to you." John 12:26 (NIV): "Whoever serves me must follow me; and where I am, my servant also will be. My Father will honor the one who serves me." Acts 20:35 (NIV): "It is more blessed to give than to receive."

27 Galatians 5:22–23 (NIV): "But the fruit of the Spirit is love, joy, peace, forbearance, kindness, goodness, faithfulness, gentleness and self-control."

28 BrainyQuote.com. "Rabindranath Tagore Quotes." https://www.brainyquote.com/quotes/ rabindranath_tagore_134933.

29 BrainyQuote.com. "Ralph Waldo Emerson Quotes." https://www.brainyquote.com/ quotes/ralph_waldo_emerson_101236.

30 Goodman, B. *Why Young People Leave WELS (Wisconsin Evangelical Lutheran Synod): National Survey of Pastors, Young Adults Leaving WELS, and Focus Group of Young Adults* (2005, September), 54.

31 Rainer, T. *The Myth of Freedom* (2007) quoted in *REACH: A Quarterly Newsletter for WELS Youth Workers* (2008, Fall), 3.

32 Barna, G. "Research Shows That Spiritual Maturity Process Should Start at a Young Age," Family & Kids (2003, November 17). https://www.barna.com/research/research-shows-that-spiritual-maturity-process-should-start-at-a-young-age.

33 Doll, R. "Shall We Close the Sunday Schools?" Christianity Today (1959, August 31). https://www.christianitytoday.com/ct/1959/august-31/shall-we-close-sunday-schools.html.

34 Isaiah 55:11 (NIV): "So is my word that goes out from my mouth: It will not return to me empty, but will accomplish what I desire and achieve the purpose for which I sent it."

35 Barna, G. "58% of Highly Engaged Christian Parents Choose a Church with Their Kids in Mind," Family and Kids (2020, January 30). https://www.barna.com/research/children-church-home.

36 Barna, G. "New Research Explores the Long-Term Effect of Spiritual Activity among Children and Teens," Family and Kids (2009, November 16). https://www.barna.com/ research/new-research-explores-the-long-term-effect-of-spiritual-activity-among-children-and-teens.

37 Ehlke, R. *The People's Bible-Proverbs* (Northwestern Publishing House, Milwaukee, WI, 1991), 213.

38 Capehart, J. *Touching Hearts, Changing Lives: Becoming a Treasured Teacher* (Group Publishing, Inc. Loveland, CO, 1999), 21.

39 Psalm 139:14 (NIV): "I praise you because I am fearfully and wonderfully made; your works are wonderful, I know that full well."

40 Cynthia Tobias. *The Way They Learn* (Focus on the Family Publishing, Colorado Springs, CO, 1994), 90.

41 From Warren, R. *Better Together: What on Earth Are We Here For?* (Purpose Driven Publishing, Lake Forest, CA, 2004), 179.

42 Quote Fancy.com. "Ralph Waldo Emerson Quotes." https://quotefancy.com/quote/893761/Ralph-Waldo-Emerson-Every-great-institution-is-the-lengthened-shadow-of-a-single-man-His.

43 Forbes.com, "100 Best Quotes on Leadership." https://www.forbes.com/sites/kevinkruse /2012/10/16/quotes-on-leadership/?sh=4b7c139c2feb.

44 Forbes.com, "100 Best Quotes on Leadership." https://www.forbes.com/sites/kevinkruse/ 2012/10/16/quotes-on-leadership/?sh=4b7c139c2feb.

45 "For such a time as this" are the words Mordecai spoke to Esther in Esther 4:14 to remind her that God provides those he needs to accomplish his will at the right time.

46 The Jesus film: https://www.youtube.com/watch?v=-Td05XH0TDg.

47 The Life of Jesus (Gospel of John): https://www.youtube.com/watch?v=T-GwlXdNewnM.

Articles for Inspiration and Encouragement

As a special "bonus," what follows on the next pages is a series of articles written by Dr. Nelson that were published as part of quarterly newsletters called *Partners* and *Sowers & Seeds*, which he produced. These newsletters for Sunday school and early childhood ministry staff had roughly ten thousand subscribers.

Shaping a Better Sunday School Culture

Every organization has a culture—the norms, values, and beliefs that underlie all the thinking, feeling, and acting that takes place within the organization. Dr. Kent Peterson, former professor of education at the University of Wisconsin–Madison and an expert on organizational culture, has said, "The organization's culture influences how people think, feel, and act. It is a key determinant of staff focus, commitment, motivation, and productivity" (Keynote address—WELS Leadership Conference, June 26, 2002).

The six elements of an organization's culture are noted below. Some Sunday school-specific "thought questions" (in italics) follow each culture element.

- The norms, values, and beliefs present
  At the very core, what does your Sunday school stand for, and how do/don't you show it? What is its mission? How do those serving in the Sunday school ministry feel and behave relative to this mission?

- Symbols and artifacts that communicate meaning
  What textual, visual, and conceptual items and ideas does your Sunday school employ to help others see who you are, what you want to be, and what you stand for? How do you help others to clearly see what your Sunday school ministry is all about?

- Stories past and present about the organization
  What is said about your Sunday school in the congregation, the community, and among the families and students served by it? What is your reputation? What do you want people to think and say about your Sunday school ministry? What reputation do you want to have?

- The relational networks that exist
  How do your Sunday school staff members, pastor, church leaders, parents, students, congregation members, and Christian elementary school staff (if your congregation also has a day school) get along and work together?

- Heroes and heroines past and present within the organization
  Who are/have been the people in your Sunday school ministry that really serve / have served as models and mentors—that help to define what your Sunday school ministry is all about? How can the rest of you learn from their example? How can you use these people and their spirit to improve what is offered?

- Rituals, traditions, and ceremonies evident
  What things does your Sunday school ministry do, both positive and negative, year after year, that have a major impact on the ministry's effectiveness? How can you accentuate the positive and eliminate the negative? What new, Christ-focused rituals, traditions, and ceremonies could be started to breathe new life and purpose into your Sunday school ministry?

As you and your Sunday school's ministry partners think about ways to improve things, let me encourage that you take some time to evaluate your Sunday school's culture. Using the bulleted phrases above, and the italicized questions, discuss the culture that exists and the culture that you really desire. Do so with a humble, open, and cooperative spirit, and let the prayer of 2 Thessalonians 1:11 be in your hearts: "With this in mind, we constantly pray...that our

God may count [us] worthy of his calling, and that by his power he may fulfill every good purpose of [ours] and every act prompted by [our] faith."

A Simple Format for Evaluation and Improvement of Your Sunday School's Culture

The simple model below can be used for any issue. The issue under consideration is placed in the left box. The two options/directions are shown with questions in the right boxes. The arrow lines and ribs represent the things you would do to achieve what the question is asking.

Begin by thinking about the issue and the left box and answering the two questions in the right boxes. After you come up with an answer that describes what things would look like under each scenario, fill in the ribs with the things that would contribute to each outcome. Once the contributors for each scenario have been identified, discuss what specific things you would do to minimize the bad and maximize the good.

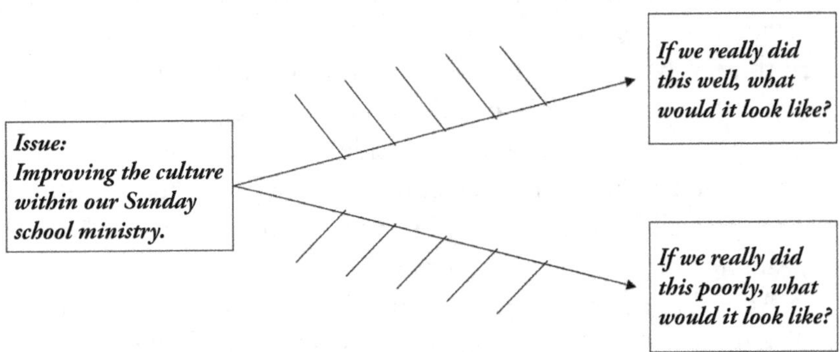

Got Stress? Get Still!

Have you ever been to a stress management workshop? If not, do you think you'd like to go to one? I went to one once. In that workshop, as in most stress management workshops, some basic questions get answered: What is stress? How do we react to stress? How can we manage stress appropriately?

One question these workshops do not cover, however, is, "How can we get rid of stress?" That question is never posed because getting rid of stress—eliminating it from our lives is, on the one hand, impossible, and on the other hand unhealthy. Can you believe that? The experts tell us that we need to have stress in our lives in order to function.

I was blessed to have had a long public ministry. As we all know, ministry at all levels can be stressful at times. As I review my ministry life, I can illustrate some of the stresses by simply recalling single sentences that were said to me.

When I was assigned to be a principal and teach seventh to eighth grades in an urban Chicago school fresh out of college, the sentence that brought a fair amount of stress to my five-year ministry there was what the Board of Education chairman said to me before my very first Board of Education meeting. This tough-looking, tough-sounding guy pulled me aside and calmly said, "Nelson, I just want you to know that if you make one mistake here, we'll nail you to the wall." I did not ask him what he meant, because I recall excusing myself to go use the bathroom.

At my second call, where I started a school and taught all eight grades for seven years, the single sentence that best illustrates the stresses of that call was also spoken to me by members of the Board of

Education, all of whom had graduate degrees in engineering, physics, computer science, and even meteorology. These highly educated men said to me, a guy with five years of experience under my belt, "Mr. Nelson, as we launch this new school, we'll really be looking to you and relying on you because you are the expert." I recall thinking, "Yeah, right!" but then realized they were dead serious. I excused myself to use the bathroom.

Seven years later, I was called to a 2,500-member congregation to be its first family minister and the second person to have such a position within the entire synod/church body at the time. The sentence that sent my stress-o-meter into the red zone was uttered by the senior pastor who also happened to be a synodical officer at the time. He said, "Joel, no one has ever done what we are asking you to do. You will be charting new territory and many other WELS congregations will be looking to us as a model." I had not yet learned where the bathrooms were, so I just swallowed hard and nodded gravely. I could cite other examples, but those three help to make the point.

Yes, there are stresses in ministry, and there are stresses in every aspect of life on this sin-filled earth. You all can share your own personal and ministerial stress stories. You all also can think of single phrases or words that trigger the stress-o-meter in your minds—that send you immediately into 911 mode.

At these times, be reminded of another single sentence that has, for me—a sometimes hyper, mostly task-centered, critically analytic personality—become one of my favorite passages from the Bible. It is Psalm 46 verse 10: "Be still, and know that I am God."

When everything around us seems to be spinning out of control, God comes to us and says, "Be still, be quiet, shhhhh. Turn to my Word and the Sacraments, and be reminded that I am in control, that I love you, that I will never take you where my unconditional love for you in Christ can't keep you." When our own personal thoughts, emotions, and feelings, make us dizzy with doubt and dread, God comes to us and says, "Be still, be quiet, shhhh. Turn to my Word and the Sacraments and be reminded that I have kept and always will keep my promises. And the greatest promise I have made and kept for you is that someday you will be with me in heaven."

Life on earth can be stressful. Sin and Satan make sure of that. But what a blessing stress is, for it helps to remind Christians that earth is not what it's all about. Because of Jesus, there is a better place waiting for us where perfect peace abounds forever and ever. And the more personally we believe that, the more willing we will be to share this Good News with all those stressed people around us who do not yet know Jesus and the peace he brings.

Sunday school ministry can be stressful in positive and negative ways. Cope better by taking the words of Psalm 46:10 to heart: "Be still, and know that I am God." Be still, be quiet, shhhh. Trust that God is there with you, for you, and in you. Then have a wonderful time!

Prayer for Inner Peace

Lord of all hopefulness, Lord of all joy,
Whose trust, ever childlike, no cares could destroy,
Be there at our waking, and give us, we pray,
Your bliss in our hearts, Lord, at the break of the day.

Lord of all eagerness, Lord of all faith,
Whose strong hands were skilled at the plane and the lathe,
Be there at our labors, and give us, we pray,
Your strength in our hearts, Lord, at the noon of the day.

Lord of all kindliness, Lord of all grace,
Your hands swift to welcome, your arms to embrace,
Be there at our homing, and give us, we pray,
Your love in our hearts, Lord, at the eve of the day.

Lord of all gentleness, Lord of all calm,
Whose voice is contentment, whose presence is balm,
Be there at our sleeping, and give us, we pray,
Your peace in our hearts, Lord, at the end of the day.

—Jan Struther (1901–1953)

If You Could Design a Sunday School

On our last Sunday school class of the year, I passed out paper and asked my seventh-grade students to respond to this question: if you could design a Sunday school class/classroom/class period, what would it look like?

Here is a representative sampling of what they wrote:

> "I would want to make students closer to Jesus and to each other. It would be more than just a Bible story. I would be getting the kids very involved and making them think."

> "Get all the kids involved with writing on the board, games, and other things for kids to participate."

> "Use games, movies, computers, and the library in our lessons."

> "I would have it be fun and exciting so people would want to come back and learn about God all the more. I would have a classroom filled with cool activities."

> "I would play some contemporary and some tra-ditional Christian songs. I would teach the lesson

the first week and then have a video to accompany the lessons the second week. If I did not use a video, I'd use games that related to the lesson."

The above are the comments of a bunch normal kids from overall good homes, and I think they gave some incredibly insightful answers. Their message is obvious: get me involved, make me think, make it exciting and fun, help me get closer to Jesus.

What do you think your students would say if you asked them this same question? Go ahead, ask them. I bet the answers would be very similar—no matter the grade level. Children want to, need to, learn in ways that truly engage them—actually all ages want and need this. And your Sunday school children want to develop a closer, more heartfelt relationship with Jesus, their classmates, and you, their teacher. They really do.

How exciting! What an opportunity! What a privilege! As a Sunday school teacher, please, please, please do everything you can to make your Sunday school classes engaging. Teach God's Word to your students in ways that make it come to life for them—and you. Read books and periodicals that offer teaching tips. Talk to the other Sunday school teachers on your staff. Tap the expertise of any Christian elementary school teachers nearby. Call public school teachers in your congregation. Get insights from your pastor. Beginning your preparation earlier is a huge help. As you look over your lesson for the upcoming Sunday and reflect on it throughout the week, you'll be surprised at the kinds of ideas that come into your mind to make your lesson connect with the visual, auditory, and kinesthetic learners in your classroom.

And two things can comfort you: (1) It's not that hard. Think about your days as a student and what you did and did not like. Put yourself into your current students' shoes and heads. Get into it yourself and you'll find a classroom of kids getting into it also. (2) God's Word has power. The Holy Spirit will do the heavy lifting, taking the Word and your lesson and working faith through it in the hearts of your students.

It's a great question to ask yourself: "If you could design a Sunday school class/classroom/class period, what would it look like?" Then realize and pledge, "Hey, I can! And I'm going to do my very best to make it one where my students are learning about Jesus in ways that make them come back again, and again, and again."

You Care as Much as I Do!

When my youngest child, Lindsay, was confirmed, it was an awesome service and very emotional for me. These kinds of things have always moved me, but in middle age, I found myself melting in the moment even faster, especially for "my baby." Worship services and ceremonies like this have as much or more impact on the parents and adults as they do on the youth. And that's how it's supposed to be, I think.

For my daughter's confirmation service, some additional "emotional enhancements" were provided. A booklet was put together containing each confirmand's name, Bible verse, parents' names, sponsors' names, and the essay each wrote on a question assigned by the pastors. Really cool was how during the actual laying on of hands by the pastor, our church's closed circuit TV system was used to project on our large, left screen the live picture of the confirmand and pastor, but from a more frontal angle, so everyone could see things better. At the same time, on the large, right screen, a digital headshot of my white-gowned daughter, taken the day before at rehearsal, was displayed with her name and confirmation Bible verse. It was one of the most tastefully done and moving experiences I have ever had in a worship setting. Nothing could top this!

But then we went home, and my daughter opened a confirmation card she was given by Mrs. B., a Sunday school teacher she had in fourth grade. In the beautiful card was a Sunday school worksheet this teacher had given and collected from my daughter almost five years earlier. On the worksheet, my young daughter wrote answers to questions about herself, her favorites, and what she felt God's blessings to her were. On the back, Mrs. B. wrote, "God's continued blessings, Lindsay. My prayer is the same for you since we studied his truths in 4th grade SS and learned how much God loves us: that you will always stay close to your Life Savior." When we passed this around, I melted some more.

Can you believe it? This Sunday school teacher kept something from my daughter (and other students too) for five years in order to present it to her on her confirmation day as a token and remembrance of godly beliefs expressed earlier and now confirmed today. What a great way to connect formative Christian education past with ongoing Christian education present and future. What a way for Mrs. B. to demonstrate to my daughter and my family that she cares as much about my child's spiritual walk as I do.

I thank the Lord for Mrs. B., for all the Sunday school teachers my children ever had, and for all the Sunday school teachers at my congregation and in my church body. You touch lives, both student and parent, with the Word and your witness. By the power of the Holy Spirit, you help keep our children committed to Christ. Thanks so very, very much for caring as much as you do!

Revitalizing Your Sunday School

In George Bernard Shaw's *Pygmalion*, the professor helps a backward and slovenly Eliza Doolittle become an elegant lady. He does this by treating her like a lady at all times until she begins to live up to his expectations of her. Goethe, the German poet and novelist, commented on expectations when he said, "Treat a man as he appears to be and you have made him worse. But treat a man as if he already were what he potentially could be, and you have made him what he should be." Expectations play an important role in the revitalization of things.

If we want to *revitalize*, or as Webster says, "give new life to," our Sunday school programs, we have to raise our expectations. We have to think of our Sunday school programs, not as what they are, but as what they potentially, with God's blessings and direction, could be.

What kind of commitment do you expect?

The Sunday school must never be looked upon as a stepchild. This is easy to do, especially if your congregation also operates a Christian elementary school. Rather, the Sunday school must be thought of as a twin, totally sharing with the church's elementary school or other youth-nurturing programs the attention, support, and prayers of the congregation and its leaders.

If the Sunday school program appears to be receiving less of these, is it the fault of the congregation? Hardly. It is the fault of the Sunday school leadership that has been unsuccessful at nurturing and strengthening whatever support is present.

Every Christian adult ought to recognize the importance of Christian training for children. And every Christian adult wants to be committed in his/her support of children. However, it may be that parishioners are not willing to support your existing program in the way you ask them to. So what do you need to do about this? You need to raise your expectations of how committed your congregation should be to the program.

Sunday school touches the lives and hearts of children.

Stress to your congregation that Sunday school gives children a great opportunity to learn about Jesus their dear Savior and friend through quality, high-interest presentations of Bible lessons and truths. Through joyful, enthusiastic, and loving teachers, Sunday school gives children a wonderful chance to see firsthand what it means to live their lives for Christ. And most important of all, Sunday school provides children with the opportunity to grow in faith.

Sunday school also touches adult lives.

There is a saying, "A believer's talents are not to be laid up for self but laid out in service." This saying can be applied to a Sunday school program because this agency provides a number of members with opportunities to use their talents to serve God and others. Adults who recognize and appreciate what God has done for them through Christ will welcome these opportunities to serve the Lord. Serving the Lord through Sunday school gives adults the opportunity to carry out the Savior's directive to go and tell. It also gives them a joyful opportunity to watch the faces and hear the voices of children speaking and singing praises to God for all that he has said and done.

Sunday school also touches the community.

A well-run and inviting Sunday school program can be one of the most effective ways for you to reach out into your community with the gospel. People who study growing churches repeatedly cite effective Sunday school as being a major contributing factor in such growth. Your Sunday school is one evidence of how outreach-minded your members are. A well-run, optimistic, Christ-centered Sunday school program speaks volumes to the community about the commitment and concern of a congregation to its mission.

Are you expecting enough?

Is your Sunday school everything it could potentially be? Probably not. There is always room for improvement. Is your congregation's commitment to your Sunday school program what it potentially could be? Probably not. We can never be too committed to the cause of Christ.

If you are a leader in your church or Sunday school program, begin to expect more from your congregation. In a loving way, remind your members that your Sunday school touches the lives and souls of your children and adults, as well as those in the community. In as many ways and as many times as you can, communicate to your congregation, your staff, your students, and your parents that the mission of Sunday school is the same mission Christ gave to the church and that your Sunday school program, under God, is going to be the best it can be. Then, as God blesses you to do so, make it happen.

Be a Leader Who Follows

The year Barack Obama ran to become president of the United States, there were eight other people officially running for president from the Democrat Party with two more mulling it over. The Republican Party also had eight candidates officially running, with four additional ones thinking about it. And just to be fair to the other political parties, there were two candidates from the Constitution Party, five from the Green Party, seven from the Libertarian Party, and fourteen independents running! All of these men and women were running because they felt they had the leadership talents and abilities required for the job.

Leadership is a huge topic of interest and study, and growing every day. Bernard Bass and Ralph Stogdill's 1974 *Handbook of Leadership* cited 3,000 books, articles, and studies on the subject. Their second edition (1981) cited 4,700 and their third edition (1990) contained 7,500 citations. A 2009 edition had over 10,000 references to books, articles, and studies on leadership.

Why is leadership such a big deal? Have you ever thought about that? I think there are two reasons: (1) everyone is impacted by some kind of leadership, and (2) everyone is a potential leader. John Gardner, an expert on leadership, expressed it this way: "Leadership is dispersed throughout all segments of the society—government, business, organized labor, the professions, the minority committees, the universities, social agencies, and so on. Leadership is also dispersed down through many levels of social functioning, from the loftiest levels of our national life down to the school principal, the local union leader, the shop supervisor."

Leadership is also a big deal because everyone is a potential leader. Alexander Astin, another leadership scholar, wrote, "A leader is anyone, regardless of formal position, who serves as an effective, social change agent, so in this sense, everyone is a potential leader."

If you had to define the word *leadership*, what would you say? One of the shortest definitions for *leadership* I ever saw was this: "Leadership is a process of influencing others to achieve a goal." I don't have to tell you that Jesus was a leader. If you Google the phrase "Jesus on leadership," you get 912,865 entries. But we really don't need to do the web search. We know Jesus was a leader, and we know he influenced others. He prayed, he preached, he taught, he performed miracles. Many came to faith and achieved the goal of life everlasting.

For me, Jesus's greatest leadership influence is seen in the way he *lived* his leadership. He was a loving, sacrificing servant. And the Bible encourages all of us leaders to be the same. In Mark 10:42–45, Jesus talks to his disciples and us about the contrast between worldly leadership and his leadership. These words are spoken after the episode where James and John lobby Jesus to set up a special seating chart in heaven: Jesus said, "You know that those who are regarded as rulers of the Gentiles lord it over them, and their high officials exercise authority over them. Not so with you. Instead, whoever wants to become great among you must be your servant, and whoever wants to be first must be slave of all. For even the Son of Man did not come to be served, but to serve, and to give his life as a ransom for many" (NIV).

The Message puts Mark 10:42–45 this way: "You've observed how godless rulers throw their weight around," Jesus said, "and when people get a little power how quickly it goes to their heads. It's not going to be that way with you. Whoever wants to be great must become a servant. Whoever wants to be first among you must be your slave. That is what the Son of Man has done: He came to serve, not to be served—and then to give away his life in exchange for many who are held hostage."

If someone—coworkers, members of your church, family, friends, people in the community, and especially fellow Sunday school staff and students—were to characterize your leadership, however it looks, whatever form it takes, would they be able to say that you are a loving servant-leader like Jesus? Or would they say you throw your weight around, and your power has gone to your head?

Dear fellow Christian leaders, keep Jesus's servant-leader model in your minds and hearts this Sunday school year and always. Pray that the Holy Spirit fills you with a personal leadership style that reflects Jesus and makes others want to learn more about him and be leaders like him, too.

If leadership is influencing others to achieve a goal, let's do all we can, with God's help, to lovingly lead our Sunday school students and their families to Jesus and eternal life forever with him. There is no greater goal.

The Way They Should Go

Probably the most quoted Bible passage to support the value of Christian education for children is Proverbs 22:6, "Train a child in the way he should go and when he is old, he will not turn from it." Recently I was reading excerpts from a book called *Touching Hearts, Changing Lives: Becoming a Treasured Teacher* by Jody Capehart (Group Publishing 1999). In one excerpt, I encountered something I have never really thought of before relative to Proverbs 22:6. Capehart talked about the phrase "in the way he should go," and indicated that these words literally mean "according to his way." She went on to say that when this passage is viewed like this, it can be an encouragement to parents and teachers to discern the individuality and special strengths that God has given each of his children.

The C. F. Keil and F. Delitzsch (1970) *Commentaries on the Old Testament-Proverbs of Solomon* adds this about the meaning of Proverbs 22:6. "The instruction of youth, the education of youth, ought to be conformed to the nature of youth; the matter of instruction, the manner of instruction, ought to regulate itself according to the stage of life, and its peculiarities; the method ought to be arranged according to the degree of development which the mental and bodily life of the youth has arrived at" (pg. 86–87).

While the main point of Proverbs 22:6 is a spiritual one, encouraging parents and others to direct youth down the path God wants them to take (Ehlke, 2001, *The People's Bible-Proverbs*, pg. 213), the secondary point is valid, and Capehart, Keil, and Delitsch express it. Proverbs 22:6 contains an encouragement to teach our students in developmentally appropriate ways that best connect with how they learn, using methods that best accommodate how God has gifted each of them.

It's an absolute fact that God's Word has all the power it needs to change hearts, and the Holy Spirit always works through that powerful Word. But many years of ministry has moved me to believe, with all my heart, that *how* we teach God's Word to our children in Sunday school (or related ministries) is extremely important. *How* we teach God's Word holds the greatest potential for keeping children in Sunday school. I also believe, with all my heart, that the same holds true for the adults in our congregations. *How* we present God's Word, to students of all ages, has a tremendous impact on how it will be received. Consider whether the following quotes apply to your situation:

> "Christian education in a majority of congregations is a tired enterprise in need of reform. Often out of touch with adult and adolescent needs, it experiences increasing difficulty in finding and motivating volunteers, faces general disinterest among its 'clients,' and employs models and procedures that have changed little over time." (Peter Benson and Carolyn Eklin, Search Institute, 1990)

> "Sunday schools [for adults and children] simply do not provide the quality of teaching and experience that people demand these days in exchange for their time." (George Barna, Ministry Currents, 1991)

> "The teachers just talk and we just sit there." (Bryan, Grade 3, Interview with Thom Schultz of Group Publishing, Incorporated, 1992)

Those quotes are real but are also really negative, so consider this quote:

> "Christian education matters much more than we expected. Of all the areas of congregational life we examined, involvement in an effective Christian education program has the strongest tie to a person's growth in faith. While other congregational factors also matter, nothing matters more than effective Christian education. And this is as true for adults as it is for children." (Peter Benson and Carolyn Eklin, Effective Christian Education: A National Study of 11,000 Adults and Youth from Protestant Congregations, Search Institute, 1990)

The seven most important words in the above quote are, "Nothing matters more than effective Christian education!" For effective Christian education—defined as education that presents the Gospel of Jesus Christ in all its truth and purity, and in ways that truly engage those who study it—prepares students for purposeful and fulfilling lives on earth, and most importantly, for glorious and eternal lives in heaven.

Dear partner, as you reflect on this article, and your current calling in Sunday school ministry, honestly ask yourself a couple of questions: (1) Does my teaching provide the most effective Christian education possible for my dear students? (2) Would the parents of my Sunday school students and the students themselves feel that my teaching is the most effective it can be?

If the answer to those questions is, "I really think so," then humbly thank the Lord for the impact he is allowing you to have. Also, do whatever you can to partner with the other members of your Sunday school ministry to improve their effectiveness. If the answer to the questions is, "I really don't think it is," then commit yourself to doing whatever it takes to steadily improve. Becoming a better teacher is a process. The journey to improvement begins with small steps.

Teaching children about Jesus is a joy and privilege. Teaching them "in the way they should go" is an absolute blast, for them and also for you!

It's Time to Talk to Parents

Mark DeVries, in *Family-Based Youth Ministry* (1994) said it so well: "Because of the extensive exposure parents have to their own children, they leave an indelible impression that radically affects how receptive their children will be to the gospel. There is overwhelming evidence that parents are, almost always, the single most significant determining factor in the development of their children."

DeVries is so correct, and most people ministering to children agree with his assessment. But why then do so many of these same ministers have such a hard time interacting with the parents of the children they teach? It's difficult to understand why ministers don't partner better with parents. Communicating with the home is soooooooooooooo important. It does so much in the way of letting the family know we care about them. It helps them to better understand how much Jesus cares for them too. And frankly, it's not that hard, hazardous, or hair-raising.

Below are some simple suggestions for when and how to communicate with the parents of children in your Sunday school or related ministry. Any kind of communication can be very powerful. A note, email, text, or card are very good. A phone call is absolutely wonderful. A home visit would be out of this world! Bottom line, communication builds relationships, and Christian relationships are a great bridge to Jesus. For the sake of this article, the communication ideas below model phone contact, although face-to-face contact could also apply.

Some Good Times to Communicate

When a child is doing really well in some way: Parents expect the worst when the teacher calls. Surprise them and really stroke their child.

Sample Phone Call: Of course, the conversation will vary as parents respond. (To the parent): "Hello, this is Joan Johnson from St. Paul's Sunday school. Susan has just been the most helpful the past few Sundays. She helps clean up without being asked, she shares with others so well. You can be so proud of her. Susan is such a precious little girl to the Lord and to all of us at Sunday school. We love having her in our class. I just wanted to share this with you. Keep up the good work!"

You could make a similar call when you know of some special "event" happening in the child's/family's life (i.e. new baby, death of a relative, big game coming up, birthday, etc.).

When a child is absent: Because of all the shared custody issues with children today, perhaps a good "rule" is to have personal contact after two to three missed Sundays (or whatever day you have sessions) in a row. You can certainly do it sooner if you like, but after three, a contact with the family would be really great. A personal as opposed to written contact would be best.

Sample Phone Call: Of course, the conversation will vary as parents respond. (To the parent): "Hello, this is Tom Weldon from Good Shepherd's Bible Hour. Justin has missed three weeks of class, and I am just calling to see if everything is all right. (Lovingly discuss whatever may come up. Offer whatever assistance you can.) Justin is such a precious child to the Lord and to all of us at Bible Hour. We love having him in our class. We hope to see him next week."

When a child is being a little stinker: Let's face it, Jesus's little lambs have Old Adams just like the grown sheep do. Most times, children "act up" because their teachers have not really engaged them in the lesson. Sometimes, however, a child just wants to stir things up. Use these "tense" times as another opportunity to minister to the home in a loving way. A face-to-face interaction would be best, but if that isn't possible, try calling. Make sure your tone of voice reflects love and concern, not anger and upset.

Sample Phone Call: Of course, the conversation will vary as parents respond. (To the parent): "Hello, this is Wendy Lipinski from Our Savior's Kids' Power Hour. I have been having some difficulty with Susan, and I was wondering if you could help me with it. Susan has been talking a lot in class and disrupting things a bit. What would you suggest I do to help her see this is not appropriate? (Let parents make suggestions. That way you are co-opting them into the issue and recognizing they know more about their child than you do.) Let me think about some of the things you suggested. Could you also talk to her about it? I am very glad that Susan is in my class. God has given her so many gifts and abilities (maybe cite some), but I am not going to allow her to disrupt the others. I am confident that all of us working together can resolve this little situation. Thanks so much for your time. I'll keep you posted, and God be with you."

Whatever the situation, positively communicating with parents (or guardians) holds great potential to connect God's people to each other, to the church, to the Word, and to Jesus.

When you talk to parents, you create an opportunity to share the Good News with them.

Everybody Wants to Be a Winner!

I love "March Madness," that time of year when high school and college basketball seasons come to a close with the loud and enthusiastic cheering of faithful and sometimes fanatical fans. Teams and cheerleading squads all over the country will ramp up their intensity and spirit.

In the annals of cheerleading, you will find two cheers that are classics. Every cheerleading squad does them because every sports team wants them. One is the tried and true, energy-charged V-I-C-T-O-R-Y. In my high school, it was the class competition cheer. The cheerleaders would yell out, "Freshmen, what's your battle cry?" and the freshmen would scream, "V-I-C-T-O-R-Y." The sophomores were next, and so on. The other classic cheer is the spirit-lifting, motivational S-U-C-C-E-S-S. In my high school, this cheer was done with a certain rhythm and action: S-u-C-c-E-s-S (clap, stomp), *success*!

Victory and success. They go together. And what team is ever considered successful if they are not also victorious if they are not winning? Our world worships winners. I mean, when was the last time you heard a cheerleading squad yell out, "Gimme an L! Gimme an O! Gimme an S! Gimme an E! What's that spell? L-O-S-E." What cheerleading squad would last if their trademark cheer was, "Try your best, and that will be OK. If you should lose, we'll love you anyway!"? Cheers like that are downright un-American. We all know that ex-pro basketball coach Bill Musselman was right. He posted this quote over his team's locker room door: "Defeat is worse than death. Because you have to live with defeat." And our culture advocates that message big time. In sports, business, politics, medicine, entertainment, the military, you name it…winning is everything. But what about Jesus?

Jesus replied, "Foxes have holes and birds of the air have nests, but the Son of Man has no place to lay his head."

(Matthew 8:20)

For you know the grace of our Lord Jesus Christ, that though he was rich, yet for our sakes he became poor, so that you through his poverty might become rich.

(2 Corinthians 8:9)

They got up, drove him out of the town, and took him to the brow of a hill on which the town was built, in order to throw him down the cliff.

(Luke 4:29)

From this time many of his disciples turned back and no longer followed him.

(John 6:66)

By the standards of his day, Jesus was not much of a success, was he? By the standards of the world today, Jesus and all of his followers should be walking around with their fingers making an "L" on their foreheads…*losers!* Why is it, however, that we don't walk around with an "L" on our foreheads? Because Jesus was *not* a loser. We know what Jesus did, and we know the horrible things that were done to him were part of God's amazing and winning game plan to rescue all mankind from sin, death, and hell. We know that Jesus was successful. His perfect life, his sacrificial death, and his glorious resurrection won the ultimate victory for all of us.

Death has been swallowed up in victory. Where, O death, is your victory. Where, O death, is your sting? The sting of death is sin, and the power of sin is the law. But thanks be to God! He gives us the victory through our Lord Jesus Christ.

(1 Corinthians 15:54–57)

Because of Jesus, we are winners! But do we live and act this way? Not enough. Our sometimes poor attitude toward parents and students, our lack of preparation and enthusiasm in our lessons, our disinterest in communicating and cooperating are not the fallout of Jesus's failure. They are the result of Jesus' followers and fans not comprehending and celebrating his victory enough, and that's a March Madness that needs to stop now.

We are winners. Jesus has won the victory. Heaven is ours. The victory parade marches on. Let's join it with more passion and let's show our students and their families what it means to us to be hooked up with *the* winner. And you know what, they will listen and they will follow. You know why? Because everybody wants to be a winner!

The Hidden Curriculum

What follows is a real conversation between a researcher and a Sunday school student. Read it, and ponder the questions beneath.

RESEARCHER: How long have you been going to church?
STUDENT: Since I was a baby.
R: How do you like your classes at church?
S: They're too much like school.
R: How's that?
S: They're boring.
R: How so?
S: We have to sit in chairs and memorize stuff.
R: What have you memorized?
S: Verses from the Bible. We get a piece of candy if we come with the verses memorized.
R: Can you say the last verse you got some candy for?
S: I don't remember.
R: Do you remember any of them?
S: No, I'm sorry.
R: Well, can you remember what any of them meant?
S: No. I guess I have a bad memory.
R: Can you tell me what it takes for a person to get to heaven?
S: Study hard.

- What's your initial reaction to the realism of this conversation?
- Could this conversation apply in your Sunday school?

- What might this conversation say about a "hidden curriculum"?
- What might you predict about this child's future in the Christian church?

The Realism of the Conversation

Did you feel that this conversation represents a pretty real situation? If you did, you'd be like hundreds of other Sunday school teachers to whom I have presented it. What is shown in this interview is, sad to say, very real. It happens all the time.

Application in Your Circles

Here again, hundreds of other Sunday school teachers have expressed that this conversation could have been recorded in their settings. Too often, our Sunday school classes look just like another day of school. Too frequently, our lessons are presented in less than engaging (spelled b-o-r-i-n-g) ways. And when it comes to Bible memory work, children focus on repeating the words without understanding their real meaning.

The Hidden Curriculum

The curriculum is the well-thought-out, organized, systematic course of study being presented to the students—what will be taught and what students are to get out of it. Sometimes, however, students "take away" something quite different than what the curriculum and its teachers intend. They learn something far removed from what is really desired. This is called the "hidden" curriculum. In too many cases, what children "learn" in Sunday school is that studying God's Word is purely an academic exercise, that knowing the facts about Jesus trumps the relationship we have with him, that Bible study is no fun, that Sunday school is not an accepting, loving, restful, peaceful, healing oasis in the week.

The Child's Future in the Church

Pondering this question is the saddest of all because the answer could very well be that this child will not have a future in the church. As soon as he is given the opportunity to decide on his own what he will do, or after he has worn his parents down enough, he will stop coming and may never return.

How would the student/researcher interview go at your Sunday school? It might be a very good discussion question for your staff to consider. Identifying strengths and weaknesses in your Sunday school ministry now can set the stage for wonderful improvement for the year ahead. Nothing is perfect, and your Sunday school ministry never will be either. But it can always improve. Pray about it, talk about it, and work at it. Then interview a student and hear, "My Sunday school and my Jesus are awesome!"

Soon, Soon It Will Be June

I coined the above phrase when I was teaching all eight grades in a one-room school. While I hate to say it, reciting that rather unspiritual and self-pity-laden mantra did help me to make it to the end of the school year sometimes. If I am going to be totally honest, I have to admit that some years I mumbled the mantra quite early—I think November was the record. "Soon, soon it will be June" may also be the phrase or thought that has helped to get you to the end of this Sunday school year. If you have been/are still mumbling that mantra, I understand, totally.

Teaching children today, even for one hour a week, can be a very draining thing, especially if you have been doing what you are supposed to be doing: thoroughly preparing well in advance; teaching a truly engaging lesson that connects with all the learning modalities; modeling an upbeat, positive, and spiritual attitude; praying for your students and their families; and personally sharing yourself and your faith with students and parents alike. If you have been doing that for several weeks/months, your teaching tank may be close to the empty mark about now. Add to that the spiritual/psychological/emotional labor invested as you contemplate the impact you are having on children who sometimes seem to have so much working against them, and you wonder how you made it this far at all.

I take turns teaching 23 seventh graders in my congregation's Sunday school. Our average attendance is 19. Our class is 50/50 Christian elementary school and public school students. Gearing up for this class and then really delivering on the weeks I teach is one of those exhilarating/exhausting things. Usually after class, I need to go home and change out of my sweaty clothes. But while pooped, and particularly so at this time of the year, I have to say it is an incredible and exciting privilege. I know you feel the same way; otherwise, you would not be as involved as you are.

It is an incredible and exciting privilege to learn more about Jesus through my personal devotion and lesson preparation. It is an incredible and exciting privilege to share Jesus with students and parents who so need his grace, mercy, and peace in their lives. At this time of the year, I want to say thank you. Thank you for being a Sunday school teacher who is sharing the gospel with children. Thank you for giving of your time, talent, and frequently your treasure to provide for your students.

We may not always see the results, but we trust God's promises that his Word works. We also have the ultimate promise that gets us through to our ultimate end: Soon, soon it will be eternity...with Jesus!

Wasn't It Great?

Wasn't teaching Sunday school great this year? Wasn't teaching God's Word exciting? What made it so great and exciting was that the lessons you taught, the words of Scripture you shared, have power to change hearts and lives for all eternity. But that's not all of it.

Teaching was great and teaching God's Word was exciting also because of the students you taught. In your classroom, you had individuals who were gifted by God in such unique and different ways. No two students were alike. No two learned the same way. Each student was truly a special piece in the puzzle of God's family. Each student saw the world through the learning style windows God decided they should have. Each student came to class with a foundation of prior knowledge that could be built upon and expanded. Every student liked to have fun while studying God's Word. Not one of them was a lifeless, ignorant, emotionless blob that had to be pounded into something worthwhile. They were abundantly worthwhile already in Jesus, just like you and me.

What a privilege you had, dear teacher, to help your students learn the real lesson: Jesus Christ is their Savior from sin, their Friend through life, and their ticket to the joys of heaven. What a privilege was yours to be used by the Holy Spirit to provide lessons and learning that made God's Word come to life in young minds and hearts.

Thanks for all you did this year! It's going to be even better next year!

What Did You Learn in School Today?

When you were a child and came home from school, invariably, there would be one question asked you by your mom or dad. In fact, this question is probably the most asked after-school question of all children everywhere. The question: "What did you learn in school today?" This universal, after-school question has an equally universal answer: "Nothing."

Both the parents that ask the universal after-school question and the kids that give the universal "nothing" answer, know that that answer is not accurate by a long shot. We are *always* learning something. From the first gulps of breath at birth to our last gasps for breath at death, we are learning.

People who are learning, whether young or old, are like branches on a plant—growing, spreading, reaching, climbing, changing. How much and how well the branches grow, however, depends on the main plant and the support and nourishment it provides the branches.

Jesus understands how important the main plant is to the branches. The Scripture text below places the plant-branch picture in our minds, and Jesus uses it to teach us a fundamental truth about being his disciples.

> "I am the vine; you are the branches. If a man remains in me and I in him, he will bear much fruit; apart from me you can do nothing."

In these words, Jesus, the Master Discipler, reminds us that being his disciples means that we have to be firmly connected to him. And we do this through the faithful use of the Means of Grace, the Word and Sacraments. When we stay connected to Christ through the Means of Grace, we will bear much fruit—not *might*, not *can*, but *will!*

Evangelist D. L. Moody told a story about a picture he had seen that impressed him greatly and illustrated the idea of being connected to Christ. The picture portrayed a woman grasping a cross firmly with both hands as she was being rescued from a stormy sea. Moody would later tell how that picture lost much of its impact after he saw another picture. In the second picture, a woman was also being rescued from raging waters. But while clinging with one hand to the cross, her other hand was lifting another person out of the waves to safety.

That second picture dramatically portrays the lesson the Master Discipler, Jesus, wants us to learn. When we, in faith, firmly grab onto him and all he has done for us, we are then given the strength and courage to reach out and grab onto others so they too can become Christ's disciples.

In a world that's becoming increasingly dangerous, paranoid, and uncertain, it is vital that those of us who have the saving, calming, absolute truth, share it with others—help others crawl out of the raging waters of their uncertainty and unbelief and grab onto Jesus as firmly as we have.

The Master Discipler says, "I am the vine, you are the branches." What a privilege to be a Sunday school teacher who is used by the Holy Spirit to help children and their parents grab on to Jesus! Let's be good disciples. Let's be strong branches that bear abundant fruit. Let's reach out to others so they can become branches with us on the life-giving, life-saving vine of Jesus.

Don't Lose Your Way

One summer, my family took a camping trip through northern CA, Oregon, and Washington. We had just purchased a new minivan and thought the trip would be a good test of it. One night, we wanted to get to a certain campsite before dark. My wife noticed that the map showed a shortcut to the campsite. The shortcut was labeled "unimproved highway." The map key defined this as "more gravel than asphalt." My wife said, "Let's take it." I asked, "How long of a stretch is it?" She said, "About 28 miles, but it will save us an hour." I said, "Let's go for it."

The unimproved highway was really great—for the first five miles—and then it got bumpier and narrower and dustier. After five more miles, I made the executive decision to turn off the air conditioner because I didn't think the dust being sucked into my new van's air conditioning was a good idea. We opened the windows, as it was about 85 degrees outside, but the dust was coming in so much, I told everyone to close them.

After five more miles, the road narrowed to one lane, and we were going about 11 miles an hour to minimize the dust cloud created by the van. Drenched in perspiration, I asked, "Does it seem a bit odd that we haven't seen any other cars on this road?" I am sure my wife suggested that we turn around, but being a man and committed to the plan we had devised, I said, "No…anyway, how would I turn around?" I asked my wife. "Perhaps you haven't noticed, honey, but the road you picked for us has been one lane for the last three miles, and tree branches have been scraping both sides of the van."

At this point, my son who was four years old, asked, "Dad, are there any mountain lions in these woods?" My response was short and to the point: "Be still, son. When Mom selected this great route for us, she probably also figured out how we can fight them off."

Well, to make a long story longer, after two more miles, the conversation between driver and navigator had become a bit more heated in more ways than one. We had 13 miles to go, which was too far to go under these conditions. We had gone 15 miles already, too far to try and drive in reverse. I stopped the car and my wife and I squared off in a hot, sweaty, verbal donnybrook that would have scared away any mountain lion within a 25-mile radius.

At one of the breath-catching pauses in the argument, my daughter, who was 6 years old at the time, said from the back seat, "Mommy and Daddy, don't you think we should be praying about this?" Our arguing stopped dead. Out of the mouth of a babe, two sweaty, sinful, and ashamed adults were rebuked.

We did pray, right then and there, for forgiveness, for patience, for protection, and guidance. And then we slowly stared down the road again. A mile further, we came upon another road that was not on the map but was wider and looked more traveled. We took it and were led back to the main highway. We were saved!

Later that night, as we sat by our campfire, we talked about how the Lord had shown us the way when we seemed so lost. The Lord showed us the way out when we were lost in the woods, and he shows us the way out from being lost in our sins. We read John 14:6, "Jesus answered, 'I am the way and the truth and the life. No one comes to the Father except through me.'" John 14:6 is not news to any of us. We know with all of our hearts that Jesus is the Way, the Truth, and the Life. We know what he has done for us and how good inside we feel about it. We know that someday we will be in heaven where no one is lost, where no roads are unimproved, but all are paved with gold.

Dear Sunday school teacher, enjoy your vacations and whatever fun trips you may be taking. And never lose the memory of the times when you have been lost. Without a sense of what being lost is like, you will not be fully able to identify and empathize with those around you whose souls are still lost. And unless you can identify, even a little, with those who are lost spiritually, you won't be the best Sunday school teacher you can be.

Will You Raise the Bar?

When do you start thinking about the next Sunday school year? When does your Sunday school team do its planning? As a staff pondering your Sunday school ministry for a new year, are you reflecting on what worked and didn't during the past year? Can you identify key areas to improve? Will you strategize on how to make Sunday school (or related) ministry in your setting better? Are you planning to raise the bar?

No matter the condition of your Sunday school ministry, there is always room for improvement. Do whatever you can during the summer to make the fall launch the best it can be and better than last year. If your Sunday school superintendent/leader doesn't seem to be thinking very far ahead, you, as an individual "player" need to become a loving, respectful "squeaky wheel" *now*! Your congregation's dear children and families and the Sunday school ministry that serves them are too important to let advanced planning slide.

Consider:

- What will we do to make the staff stronger and better-equipped teachers before we start the new Sunday school year and then during the year?
- How will we improve the communication of/to all stakeholders: pastor, teachers, parents, students, elected Christian education leaders, congregation members, community?
- What will we do to develop a more supportive and accountable Sunday school team?

- How can we excite more individuals, representing more age groups, to become our partners and join the Sunday school ministry?
- How can we create a more welcoming, friendly, fun Sunday school culture for students, families, and staff?
- What could we do to get parents more engaged in Sunday school and their children's Christian education?
- How will we maintain staff energy and commitment as the year goes on?
- How will we maintain student/family commitment as the year goes on?
- What should we do in spiritual ways to improve ourselves and our Sunday school ministry?

Pondering these questions now will get the Sunday school improvement ball rolling faster and farther. It will also raise the bar of ongoing, faith-filled, gospel-motivated ministry to Jesus's dear children. Enjoy your time off. Enjoy more your planning for the new Sunday school year.

It's Unconditional!

Deep lies the drift across the drive.
I know what must be done.
I boldly grab the shovel,
And hand it to my son.

Soon (for those of us stuck in "wages of sin" climates), the snow will start to fly. We will have to start plowing and scooping and piling. I don't fret the snow as much because I have children who want to go places, buy things, and live the all-around "good life." In order to live such a life in winter, my children know that, if they shovel some snow, their father will be more loving, kind, and generous. Sure, it's conditional love on my part, but that snow needs to get moved!

Praise God that conditional love is not what the heavenly Father is all about. This time of the year shows us that big time. Soon, we will focus on Jesus's birth, the human fulfillment of how wide and long and high and deep God's love for us is (Ephesians 3:18). At this time of year, we have the opportunity to learn again what God's unconditional love means to us personally, for our students and their families, for our congregation and our community. Through the Word and Sacrament, we remind ourselves of God's love for us in Christ, and our hearts overflow with joy and contentment. We are empowered by the Holy Spirit to be better teachers, better servants, better people – not just during the holidays, but always.

This holiday, as you teach the Christmas story, as you rehearse for children's services, as you worship together with your family, your students and their families, and with your congregational family, think about God's amazing love for you and all mankind.

I'd like to wish you a very blessed holiday season. It is also my prayer that your Sunday school ministry joyfully radiates to others the unconditional love of God that you have been so blessed to receive. Happy holidays!

Sinners or Saints?

In a Bible study offered in my home congregation, the question was posed to participants: "Do you see yourself as a sinner or a saint?" Without a whole lot of hesitation, almost everyone in the group said, "Sinner." The group discussed the reasons for this answer and basically concluded that this is how we have most often been taught, consciously and subconsciously, to view ourselves. There is nothing necessarily wrong with that, for truly we are all sinners. Then the study shared parts of a paper written by a pastor serving in Idaho, and the entire Bible study group was encouraged to think of themselves quite differently—as saints! The study shared information that was truly interesting and incredible! The pastor wrote,

> Over the past few years, I have been paying careful attention to how the Bible, and especially the New Testament, speaks to and about believers… To put it mildly, I have been startled at how positively the Bible speaks to and about believers…. Could the way we be addressing our members— the words we use, the emphases we make, the nature we address—could the way we speak to them be contributing to a stunting of their spiritual growth?… But what is even more startling is how the biblical writers talk to and about believers. Here's my unofficial and incomplete listing:
>
> Righteous—approximately 180 times
> Brothers—98 times just in Paul's letters

Saints—67 times
Holy—36 times
Friends—24 times in the epistles
Chosen—23 times
Children of God—13 times
Elect—10 times
Heirs—8 times
Sanctified—6 times
God's temple—5 times
Worldly or unspiritual—4 times
Wretched—2 times (Romans 7:24, Rev. 3:17)
Sinner—2 times (1 Timothy 1:15, Psalm 25:8)
Sinful—1 time (Luke 5:8)

What are we to conclude from all this? Allow me to make a few observations. The first is that, by commonly referring to believers as sinners, we are speaking in a way that confuses believers' dual nature with their single status. The Bible plainly states that believers have a dual nature - most often described as flesh and spirit. But the Bible also clearly emphasizes the believer's one status before God. We are righteous; we are saints; we are God's children; we are the heirs of heaven, and so forth. Do we speak as carefully as the Bible does?

My "takeaway" from this Bible study was that we are all still sinners, but if God's people understood better and focused more on the fact that they are also saints and heirs of heaven, their outlook, attitudes, demeanor, actions, and sense of purpose in life would be much more joy-filled, positive in direction, and inviting to others.

Sinner or a saint? What would your students answer? Do your students leave your class with head held high and total victory in their step? Do they understand that they are indeed saints because of what Jesus has done for them? Do they know, with all their hearts, that heaven is truly theirs? Do they go home to live with a positive and "heavenward" view? Is their joy in Jesus clearly and immediately evident to all? If not, you might want to remind them—and yourself—that in Christ, our sins are gone. We truly are saints!

Ministry in a Sunday
School Is a Team Effort

In business and industry, the past decade has witnessed the development and expansion of Human Resources departments because the people of any company or organization are a vital asset that must be managed conscientiously and cared for well or else the endeavor founders. When it comes to the ministry of a Sunday school, human resources matter too. The people most directly involved—pastor, superintendent/coordinator, teachers—have a dramatic impact on how well things will go. Certainly, it is the Holy Spirit that produces the results, but experience suggests that the "success" of a Sunday school is closely tied to the team spirit of the staff.

Because of sin, we know that members of any ministry team can lose focus on the big picture, lose interest in spiritual and professional growth, lose heart for ministry, lose a caring attitude for each other and those being served. If a Sunday school's ministry team is going to effectively carry out the task given to it by God, it must commit itself to a team effort that does the following:

Focuses the ministry team on the God-
appointed mission of the Sunday school

The Sunday school, in close partnership with the Christian home and congregation, exists to make disciples by sharing the Good News of Jesus Christ (Matthew 28:19–20). That is its mission. Using God's Word and by the power of the Holy Spirit, the Sunday school trains its young disciples to clearly see Jesus, dearly love him, closely follow him, and confidently share him. A team approach to ministry nurtures a stronger commitment to share Jesus Christ through the Sunday school.

Encourages the ministry team to care for each of its members

Love one another (John 13:34). Honor one another (Romans 12:10). Encourage one another (Hebrews 10:25). Accept one another (Romans 15:7). Submit to one another (Ephesians 5:21). Be devoted to one another (Romans 12:10). Speak to one another with psalms, hymns, and spiritual songs (Ephesians 5:19). Instruct one another (Romans 15:14). Spur one another on (Hebrews 10:24). Admonish one another (Colossians 3:16). Bear with one another in love (Ephesians 4:2). These familiar "one-anothering" passages from God's Word provide a good answer to the question, "Why do we need to think about Sunday school as a team ministry?" for in the largest sense, they define what team members are to do: care for each other.

A team attitude helps the members of the Sunday school ministry recognize that they are all sinners who have been graciously redeemed by the blood of Jesus. It also reminds the members of the Sunday school team that, by the power of the Holy Spirit, they can truly live as the body of Christ, accepting that each team member has been gifted by God just the way he wants them to be in order to do the work he has determined for them to do at this place and time (1 Corinthians 12).

Assists the ministry team to improve and grow

The Bible has much to say about doing everything to God's glory (2 Corinthians 5:14–15, Colossians 3:17), serving him faithfully (1 Samuel 12:24, 1 Corinthians 4:2), doing things in a proper way (1 Corinthians 14:40, Colossians 2:5), and serving others selflessly (Galatians 5:13, Philippians 2:4). Applying the truths of these passages with an eye on improving and growing as minister-teachers will cause every member of the Sunday school team to love each other, pray for each other, and work together.

Reminds the ministry team to train the whole child

Sunday school teachers and aides understand that the whole person (mind-body-soul) must be trained and nurtured to do all things to the glory of God. When a Sunday school's ministry team views its students and each other in this holistic way, and adjusts its curriculum and activities to stress this, everyone grows.

Ministry in a Sunday school is a team effort. Do all you can to make your Sunday school staff a competent, committed, and caring group of partners.

Welcome to Funday School

Did you see it? A recent issue of *TIME* magazine carried an article about the changing face of Sunday school ministry in America. The article was titled "The New Funday School" and discussed what churches are doing to "woo the Nickelodeon generation." One minister (Tom) drives his truck through a working-class Texas neighborhood and conducts a "Sidewalk Sunday School" that looks more like street theater than organized religion. In fact, the "Sunday" school actually takes place on Thursdays. The crazy antics and water balloon tosses may seem a little over the top, but Tom's philosophy is worth pondering a little. He says, "You've got to make it fun, or it's just more dry religious stuff."

Some churches, the article says, have "updated their facilities with computer stations for playing video games like *Bible Grand Slam* and movie theaters for features like *The Creation*, narrated by Amy Grant. Teachers are baking unleavened bread as they read *Exodus* and aiming slingshots at large bottles for a hands-on study of David and Goliath." Other examples find toddlers setting up a mini altar with small candles, prayer books, and Bibles for "church services," or students using "bang and clang" instruments to dramatize the storm that nearly drown the prophet Jonah. And what is the result? Listen to these quotes:

> "When I was sitting here before," said one student, "I used to bring something to do, like draw. Now I'm learning things."

"The more kids touch and they hear and they feel," said one program director, "the more likely the content becomes not only interesting, but they comprehend and understand."

"If a kid comes home and says, 'I met some kids, I had fun and loved it, and I want to go back,'" says one pastor, "most of the time the parent will say, 'OK' and return to that church.' There are church-wide benefits to a thriving children's ministry."

Like with anything else, doing what pleases God and maintaining balance is the key. The apostle Paul said it well when he was inspired to write, "'Everything is permissible'—but not everything is beneficial. 'Everything is permissible'—but not everything is constructive... So whether you eat or drink or whatever you do, do it all for the glory of God" (1 Corinthians 10:23, 31). But when it comes to what is permissible and beneficial to truly engage children in the Bible lessons you teach, there really is a lot of room for Christian creativity.

How could music be a part of the lesson, either to illustrate a special setting, demonstrate something about the culture and times, or set a special mood before or after the lesson is presented? How might playing some soft, spiritual music while students pray silently or journal their thoughts about how the truths of the lesson apply to them today enhance your teaching?

What physical movements could be incorporated into the lesson? For example, in a lesson about God giving the Law on Mt. Sinai, have students come to the front and use their faces and bodies to show the fear the Israelites must have felt when they heard the thunder from the mountain—but without making a sound! In the lesson of Creation, have students physically show (mime) how different plants and animals might have come forth at the command of God.

How might the professional mourners have shrieked and moaned at the young man of Nain's funeral? How might the father from the Parable of the Lost Son have cried, "This son of mine was dead and is alive again; he was lost and is found!" How could you make the smashing sound of the clay jars used when Gideon's army attacked the Midianites?

How might students draw or diagram portions of the lesson while you tell it or immediately after a lesson section has been completed? Students could then present their pictures to each other and discuss what they have drawn.

Of course, anything you do in the classroom should be age, as well as socially, appropriate, and it should never compromise student safety. But don't be afraid to experiment. Students of *all* ages, whether they let on or not, appreciate these things being done. And it is an absolute fact: learning occurs best when lessons are fun.

Maybe the custodian won't let you cover the entire church basement floor with white paper pieces to represent the manna in the wilderness, but you can make your lessons and your Sunday school (or similar ministry) a lot more engaging in a variety of ways. If you do, don't be surprised if your students go home and tell their parents, "I loved Funday…I mean…Sunday school today!"

Start the Year with an Excellent Question

If someone were to ask you, a teacher of God's Word, "Why do you want to teach God's Word well?" what would you answer? It's an excellent question, isn't it? In fact, it's perhaps the best question a teacher of God's Word can ask before beginning any Bible lesson preparation. "Why do I want to teach God's Word well?"

Why do I want to teach God's Word well? The number one answer is that it is *God's* Word. It is the only source of absolute truth. In a world where the black and white of right and wrong have been replaced by a sprawling area of gray, children and their families need to know that there *is* a source of truth that can be their foundation and guide for life. The words of the true God, the perfect and powerful Creator of the universe, the all-knowing, all-loving Savior are indeed right, true, and worthy of our respect, obedience, and study. Psalm 86:11 says, "Teach me your way, O LORD, and I will walk in your truth; give me an undivided heart, that I may fear your name."

Why do I want to teach God's Word well? A second reason is that it is the Word of Life. The Bible is the only book that contains the answer to the vital question, "How can I be saved?" The answer is Jesus Christ. He, and he alone, is the Way, the Truth, and the Life. Unless children and their families learn of Jesus, they cannot—absolutely cannot, be saved. The Good News of Jesus suffering, death, and resurrection must be told. The story of salvation, revealed in the pages of Scripture, is what the world needs to hear. Without that Good News, souls will be lost forever in the fires of hell. John 20:31 says, "These were written that you may believe that Jesus is the Christ, the Son of God, and that by believing you may have life in his name."

Why do I want to teach God's Word well? A third answer is that it is what God has commanded us to share. From the time he ascended into heaven, Jesus has given all Christians the clear directive to share the Good News with others. For those in the public ministry or given a special call by a congregation to teach, fulfilling Christ's command to share the Good News of the gospel is a unique privilege. For all believers, and especially for teachers of God's Word, the Great Commission recorded in Mark 16:15–16 provides the marching orders: "Go into all the world and preach the good news to all creation. Whoever believes and is baptized will be saved, but whoever does not believe will be condemned."

Why do we want to teach God's Word well?
It is *God's* Word.
It is the Word of Life.
It is what God has commanded us to share.
What more reasons could we want?

Early Childhood Education Matters

Second to the education and involvement of parents themselves, early childhood education holds the greatest potential for effecting lasting results in an array of ways.

In its *Ten Tips for Raising Happier, Healthier Children* (2002), the I Am Your Child Foundation, a national nonprofit organization dedicated to raising awareness about the importance of early childhood development and school readiness, emphasized how, "Experiences that fill [a child's] first days, months, and years have a decisive impact on the structure of a child's brain and, in turn, on every aspect of a child's life throughout adulthood."

Great Beginnings: The First Years Last Forever (1998), a collaborative project of the Wisconsin Council on Children and Families, noted that, "Childhood experiences act as the primary architects of the brain's capabilities for a lifetime. Consistent, nurturing, structured, and enriched experiences lead to a flexible, empathetic, and intelligent adult."

One of the most important parts of a child's development is what's called, identity formation—a child constructing a clear understanding of him/herself. *Early Childhood Development: A Multi-Cultural Perspective* (2000) notes: "The roots of identity can be traced to a child's early years. Young children come to view themselves as members of a family, as siblings, and as sons or daughters...Piece by piece, the child's picture of self comes into focus. Gender and ethnic identity are two significant self-discoveries that occur during the early years. Children quickly realize that they are boys or girls, and come to understand the behaviors, expectations, and status that accompany each gender. They also come to view themselves as members of an ethnic group."

Commenting on spiritual development in children, Christian researcher, George Barna, wrote, "[A] person's moral foundations are generally in place by the time they reach age nine. While those foundations are refined and the application of those foundations may shift to some extent as the individual ages, their fundamental perspectives on truth, integrity, meaning, justice, morality, and ethics are formed quite early in life" (*Transforming Your Children Into Spiritual Champions*—2003).

The above quotes (and these are just the tip of the iceberg) certainly emphasize that early childhood education matters. The Bible, Source of all Wisdom and Truth, also stresses how important the early years are. In Deuteronomy 19:18–20, God instructed parents to, "Fix these words of mine in your hearts and minds; tie them as symbols on your hands and bind them on your foreheads. Teach them to your children, talking about them when you sit at home and when you walk along the road, when you lie down and when you get up. Write them on the doorframes of your houses and on your gates." The most famous Bible passage about the benefits of Christian education, Proverbs 22:6 says, "Train a child in the way he should go, and when he is old he will not turn from it."

As you share Jesus with all of the families to whom you minister, remember that (1) early childhood education matters, and that (2) Christian education begun at the earliest stages of a child's life, with parents and church partnering together, matters eternally.

A Child's Value...Priceless!

Harold J. Morowitz, a biochemist at Yale University, once received a humorous birthday card that said, "According to biochemists, the materials that make up the human body are only worth 98 cents." Morowitz didn't believe it and began to check it out. After determining what chemicals were in the human body and what percentages of each were present, Morowitz concluded that a gram of human being was worth $245.54. He then multiplied that number by his body weight and arrived at the figure $6,000,015.44.

Though an impressive amount, Morowitz knew this figure only showed the value of body chemicals in isolation, not put together and functioning. After a few more calculations, putting molecules, cells, tissues, organs, and systems into the picture, Morowitz raised the worth of a human being to 6 quadrillion dollars. It was a mind-boggling number, but it still didn't take into account all the different things a human body can do, say, think, and feel. Finally, Morowitz exclaimed, "Each human being is truly priceless."

Amazing as that may seem, that's not even the whole story. Each one of us is more than just a magnificently designed living creature. God has given us an immortal soul. We can define soul as "the spiritual being which, when united with a body, makes a living, human person." An amazing body, an immortal soul. Can it get any better? It can, but only if we understand two other things about children and ourselves. We are sinful, and we are saved.

We are sinful. Psalm 51:5 says, "Surely I was sinful at birth, sinful from the time my mother conceived me." Romans 3:23 says, "All have sinned and fall short of the glory of God." Our wonderful body is corrupted by sin. It will die (Romans 6:23) and, left in sin, our body and soul will spend an eternity in hell (Matthew 10:28). There is nothing we can do to change this either. Nevertheless, it has been changed for us.

We're saved! "For God so loved the world that he gave his one and only Son, that whoever believes in him shall not perish but have eternal life." Jesus came into our world to save us. (Isn't it interesting that God chose to send our Savior into the world as a child?) He set you, me, and everyone else free from the slavery of sin and gave us the hope and joy of eternal life.

Harold J. Morowitz used the number 6 quadrillion dollars to try to express a person's worth. God profoundly increased the value of human worth when he lovingly sacrificed his only Son on behalf of every person who has ever lived, lives, or will live. The children and families you serve are among those for whom God's personal love-offering was given. Those complex little human bundles you teach, and their dear families cost God everything so that their ugly stains of sin could be washed clean. Those same children and families, because of the Holy Spirit working through the Word taught and modeled in your early childhood ministry, will someday receive the inheritance of a lifetime, an eternal place in heaven, living and ruling in glory with the risen and ascended Lord Jesus. You'll receive it right along with them. Talk about priceless!

Free the Children

It's a funny picture in a scary sort of way. A child (let's call her Penny) weighed down with activities and commitments to the point where she can't even navigate. Her confused, confounded look and her t-shirt say it all: "I'm a kid!" I'm just a little kid!

If you are responsible for young children (yours or others), maybe it's time that you pondered Penny's predicament and encouraged others, like Penny's parents/guardians, to do the same. Consider the following quotes:

> A child is nothing like a racing car…. Souping up babies doesn't work that way. The child is what she is. There is a certain irreducible if elusive core. Pushing, pulling, stretching, and shrinking will not really change it. There may

be spectacular interim results. The baby may say the alphabet before she walks, master two-times or even ten-times table at three. In the long run, however, this forced precocity tends to be irrelevant.... Whatever gains there are become unimportant. The losses can be irrevocable. Stella Chess (20th century), US psychiatrist, and Jane Whitbread (20th century), US writer. *Daughters,* ch. 2 (1978).

[Children] need time to stare at a wall, daydream over a picture book, make mud pies, kick a ball around, whistle a tune or play the kazoo—to do the things today's adults had time to do when they were growing up. Leslie Dreyfous (20th century), US author. AP article appearing in *The New Bedford* (MA) *Standard-Times* (February 9, 1992).

Children who are pushed into adult experience do not become precociously mature. On the contrary, they cling to childhood longer, perhaps all their lives. Peter Neubauer (20th century), US psychoanalyst. As quoted in *Children without Childhood,* by Marie Winn, 1981, ch. 13.

It's a hurried world out there. But kids still need time just to be kids. They need time to enjoy their immaturity. David Bjorklund (20th century), US child development expert. As quoted by Leslie Dreyfous, AP article in *The New Bedford* (MA) *Standard-Times* (February 9, 1992).

Experts have been studying the growing stress and disappearing downtime of modern children for quite a while. And the negative trends extend across class and region. Why are we pushing our children so far, so fast? The combination of split-up homes, double shifts, shrinking vacations, fear of boredom, need to stay competitive, wanting our cake and eating it too, all conspire to clog adult and kid schedules. And there is no let up in sight. Even summer has become more crazy than lazy and hazy. There is math camp, weight camp, leadership camp, band camp, sports camp, computer camp, church camp, etc, etc. as though summer (and the rest of the year) were about perfecting ourselves, when in fact the opposite may be true. And what's the fallout of the hurried and harried life? Look at this list of "outcomes of childhood stress" complied from several sources on the subject:

- Teen suicide and homicide rates have tripled from twenty years ago
- Childhood obesity is up 50%
- US teen pregnancy rates are the highest for any Western society
- SAT scores are plummeting
- 15–20% of children flunk kindergarten
- Millions of children are medicated to be more "manageable"
- Creativity in children is diminished
- Chronic, psychosomatic complaints on the rise: headache, stomachache, chest pain, hyperactivity, sadness, lethargy, lack of motivation
- Inability to say "no" to more impossible demands
- Foundational values, beliefs, morality, and faith are not taught from parents
- Children feel incompetent and lack self-worth
- Trouble sleeping
- Loss of appetite
- Procrastination
- Acting up
- Growing resentment that overflows in middle school and high school years
- Increased irritability and moodiness
- Higher incidence of anxiety or panic attacks
- Allergic reactions: eczema and asthma

- Hopelessness and depression
- Compulsive exercise
- Addictions: alcohol, drugs, eating disorders

As ministers who care deeply about your children and their families, you are positioned in a spot where you can lovingly raise the issue of childhood stress and its fallout with the parents and families you serve. You can also lead these parents and families to ponder what God's Word says on the subject and help them to see how perfect peace rests with Jesus.

- "My times are in your hands" (Psalm 31:15).
- "Seek the Lord while he may be found" (Isaiah 55:6).
- "It is time to seek the Lord" (Hosea 10:12b).
- "What I mean brothers, is that the time is short…for this world in its present form is passing away" (1 Corinthians 7:29–31).
- "Trust in him at all times, O people; pour out your hearts to him, for God is our refuge" (Psalm 62:8).
- "For anyone who enters God's rest also rests from his own work, just as God did from his" (Hebrews 4:10)
- "Ask where the good way is, and walk in it, and you will find rest for your souls" (Jeremiah 6:16).
- "Come unto me, all you who are weary and burdened, and I will give you rest" (Matthew 11:28).

Your encouragement and the Holy Spirit working through God's Word may help your parents and families to make needed changes as they better understand that BUSY frequently means Being Under Satan's Yoke.

Who's Pulling Your String?

In many parts of the country, spring weather includes some breezy days. Pictures of this time of year, especially if they include children, will show kites flying in the wind.

Have you ever flown a kite? Growing up in rural Wisconsin, I remember some great, spring excitement when my brother and I chased a green dragon kite—one we purchased with our own money—across an entire cornfield and into a woods when it broke loose from its string. The kite was lodged beyond our reach in the branches of a bur oak tree. We caught our breath. We tried to climb. We sat and cried. The kite was a goner, a vivid reminder of the helplessness of two simple, country boys against the mighty power of the spring wind.

When my daughter, Lindsay, now a high school junior, was three years old, we flew a kite in an open church parking lot. The kite ascended quickly on that gusty day, and I let out almost all of the line. The kite soared almost three times higher than the church steeple. When Lindsay saw that Dad seemed to be having all the fun, she asked for a turn to hold the string. I gave it to her, and she was immediately pulled forward a couple feet. She was quite surprised by the force of the unseen wind.

Kites remind me of something a student once said in answer to the question, "If you were to describe God, what would you say?" The student answered, "God is like a kite high up in the clouds. I can't see him, but I can feel his strong pull." What an insightful response.

When you think about it, God can be described like that. We can't see him, yet we know he is there. We can't touch him, yet we feel his pull. Through Word and sacrament the power of the Holy Spirit is given to us, and we are guided to love and serve Jesus in forward and upward directions.

Perhaps this spring on a sunny, breezy day, you can take children from your ministry outside and let them feel the pull of a kite. Maybe it could become an entire family event at some park or in your own church's parking lot. After the activity, you could share how, in Christ, we are all being pulled closer and closer to heaven.

Conduits for Christ

Christian teacher is…

A *mind* through which Christ *thinks.*
A *voice* through which Christ *speaks.*
A *heart* through which Christ *loves.*
A *hand* through which Christ *helps.*

The words above, adapted from *Uncle Ben's Quotebook* (1980), are a fitting reminder of what you are. In your early childhood ministry, you are a "conduit for Christ." Your mind, voice, heart, and hands are used by the Holy Spirit to pass on Jesus to the children you serve and their families.

In 1990, Peter Benson and Carolyn Eklin of the Search Institute surveyed 11,000 adults and youth from churches in several denominations, and wrote, "Christian education matters much more than we expected. Of all the areas of congregational life we examined, involvement in an effective Christian education program has the strongest tie to a person's growth in faith. While other congregational factors also matter, nothing matters more than effective Christian education, and this is as true for adults as it is for children."

The seven most important words in that quote are these: nothing matters more than effective Christian education. You and I know that, and every day we see that as the Holy Spirit, through the Good News of Jesus Christ, molds the hearts and lives of the children and families we serve. The Benson/Eklin quote also reminds us that Christian education is for *all* ages. And that's what's so amazing about where God has placed you. You are engaged in a ministry where children *and* their parents can be touched by God through you—where you can be a conduit for Christ to the entire home at a point in the family life cycle when everyone is more willing to hear what you have to say.

Take advantage of that, be intentional, ponder new and better ways to become a sharper mind through which Christ thinks, a louder voice through which Christ speaks, a bigger heart through which Christ loves, and a stronger hand through which Christ helps.

Are We There Yet?

Will you be taking a trip this summer? God willing, my family will go to "the Thumb" of Michigan to visit my wife's family in Pigeon. My in-laws actually live on Sand Point, which is a peninsula that sticks out into the Saginaw Bay of Lake Huron. It is a very beautiful setting, right on the water. The problem is, it takes 9 hours to get there by car from where we live near Milwaukee, and that's if you can get through the Chicago/Gary juggernaut quickly.

I love my wife and her family dearly, but I have told my children on more than one occasion – usually when we are into the 7th sweaty, smelly hour of our long trip to Pigeon—that when they start looking for a life mate, they might want to look closer to home.

When you take a long trip like this, especially if you have children along, you have to be prepared. You need to pack something for the kids to do…books, maybe some games, some pillows, of course, they bring their own electronic gizmos, and also plenty of food. Food is a must because as soon as anyone starts to whine, "Are we there yet?" you can shove a bunch of crackers in their mouth. I will not take this trip to MI unless I have my own personal bag of Chewy Chocolate Chip Cookies. Doing all these things during a long journey does help to keep everyone occupied, but most of the time, when you finally get to your destination, you have a headache, a stomachache, or both.

Talking about long, summer vacation journeys makes me think about another journey that seems to be taking way too long. It's the trip to heaven. I don't know about you, but there are a lot of times when I kind of whine, "Are we there yet?" I can't wait to get to heaven. It's going to make beautiful Sand Point, MI, look like a desolate, deserted, weed-infested wasteland. And just like on a long earthly trip, I can whine all I want about getting to heaven, but that's not going to get me there any faster. I won't get to heaven until God sees fit to end my earthly journey.

What's cool though is that God has given me some really great things to do to meaningfully occupy my time between now and then.

He gives me his Word to read, study, and follow.

He gives me a church to attend, to worship and praise him along with my brothers and sisters in Christ.

He gives me Christian family and friends to enjoy, do things with, to love and be loved by them.

He gives me all kinds of people to pray for and things to pray about.

He gives me countless opportunities to serve: at home, in my church, in my community.

He gives me many chances to share the Gospel with others.

He allows me to work every day with other awesome Christians.

And the things God gives me to do to occupy myself while I'm waiting to get to heaven, make me feel good, inside and out, and give me tremendous purpose, focus, confidence, and optimism. Two passages of Scripture reinforce this so well:

> But our citizenship is in heaven. And we eagerly
> await a Savior from there, the Lord Jesus Christ.
> (Philippians 3:20)

> But in keeping with his promise we are looking
> forward to a new heaven and a new earth, the
> home of righteousness. (2 Peter 3:13)

Whether the trip to heaven is still much longer for some of us, or ends while reading this article, we all know we are going to be there. And will it be great to finally be home! In the meantime, let's occupy ourselves totally with the great things God has given us to do.

All I Really Need to Know, I Learned in My Christian Preschool

Robert Fulghum wrote a book titled *All I Really Need to Know I Learned in Kindergarten*. There, Fulghum said, he learned about how to live, what to do, and how to be. He felt the sand pile of kindergarten taught him more than the mountain of graduate education. Fulghum reduced his "life learnings" to the following list:

> Share everything. Play fair. Don't hit people. Put things back where you found them. Clean up your own mess. Don't take things that aren't yours. Say you're sorry when you hurt somebody. Wash your hands before you eat. Flush. Warm cookies and cold milk are good for you. Live a balanced life—learn some and think some and draw and paint and sing and dance and play and work every day some. Take a nap every afternoon. When you go out in the world, watch out for traffic, hold hands, and stick together. Be aware of wonder. Remember the little seed in the Styrofoam cup: the roots go down and the plant goes up, and nobody really knows how or why, but we are all like that. Goldfish and hamsters and white mice and even the little seed in the Styrofoam cup—they all die. So do we. And then remember the Dick and Jane books and the first word you learned, the biggest word of all—*look*.

Fulghum's list is quite insightful and inclusive. But something is glaringly missing and any Christian preschooler could tell you what it is: Jesus loves me, this I know. That "life learning" is absolute truth and reflects total confidence. Jesus loves *me* so much that he suffered, died, and rose again, and because of it, someday I'll be in heaven. By the power of the Holy Spirit, I *know* this with every fiber of my being. This simple Bible truth is sometimes the only thing I need to get through life.

I was powerfully reminded of this while working on a video/Bible study series for parents and teens. These studies share the real-life stories of youth and families who have gone through some difficult issues. In one of the episodes, a family deals with the horrible and senseless murder of their teen daughter. As the family struggles through the tragedy the mother says what really helped to get her through was, "that little child's verse, 'Jesus loves me this I know for the Bible tells me so.'"

What a privilege you have to be able to teach "that little child's verse" to the children in your ministry. What joy is yours to know that this "life learning" is something that can carry them through the toughest times in life. What a calling you have: teaching little ones and their parents all they really need to know.

It's the Most Wonderful Time of the Year!

It won't be long before the words and music of holiday songs will be filling malls, stores, homes, and cars all over the country. Very soon, the stores you visit will have gone into full holiday mode. It is the most wonderful time of the year, isn't it? And it's really this way for your ministry, too. In the days and weeks to come, you will have many opportunities to help children and parents see why.

By the power of the Holy Spirit, you'll be able to help young, inquisitive, and absorbent minds and hearts gaze into the angel-filled night, peek into the dimly lit stable, smell the cattle and hay, hear the gentle breathing of the Son of God, and sing with all their hearts "Away in a Manger" and "Go Tell It on the Mountain." You'll be able to teach them, in ways they'll always remember, that Baby Jesus is their Savior from sin.

By the power of the Holy Spirit, you'll be able to refresh older, anxious, and filtering minds and hearts with the calming Good News, that this life's hurry, hassle, and hatred are totally healed by the Son of God who grew to die in their place. You'll be able to remind them—because it's so easy to lose focus—that Jesus, their Savior, brother, and friend, has prepared a heavenly peace for them and their children. You'll help them to sing "A Great and Mighty Wonder" like they never have before.

It is the most wonderful time of the year! And what a blessing and privilege for you to be able to share why with the children and families you serve. Do it well, from the heart, trusting that the Baby Jesus, the Son of God, is your Savior too.

Come, Join Our Family

Family studies experts say that everyone has two families: a biological family and a functional family. The "biological family" is those we are related to because of common blood or through the marriage of one of our blood relatives. This includes the nuclear or immediate family and the greater or extended family: grandparents, cousins, aunts, uncles, and in-laws. The "functional family" is those not biologically related to us that function as a family. Adopted children, foster children, unofficially adopted people who take the place of our natural kin when we are separated from them.

Being separated from biological family is very common in today's world. For some, geography is the reason, as careers and a mobile society keep family members apart for longer periods. For others, dysfunction is the reason. Family members may live in the same town, or even the same house, but cannot bring themselves to live in healthy and happy ways.

The need for family, placed in us by a loving, heavenly Father, moves many whose biological families are not there, to search out and develop functional ones. And herein lies a great mission opportunity. Your ministry and the congregation that sponsors it can become the functional family for many searchers today.

Royce Money, author of *Ministering to Families: A Positive Plan of Action* (ACU Press) wrote, "[The church] emphasizes home-centered nurture and nurture found through the church. Concern for individual families within the greater family of God is central to the church's identity and mission. The church is more like a family than anything else."

Think about that. The church is more like a family than anything else! Could your children's ministry be described this way too? If not, consider ways to become an even more welcoming and caring family in Christ to those you serve.

About the Author

Dr. Joel A. Nelson is perhaps best described via his personal mission statement: "Raise the bar with competence, creativity, care, and Christ." He has tried, with God's gracious help and blessing, to do that everywhere he has been.

Dr. Nelson served God and the church full-time in seven different positions and geographic locations over his 44-year ministry career. He was a teacher, Christian school principal (3 schools), director of family ministries, and director of youth and adult discipleship in congregations ranging from 120 to 2,800 members. He also served as associate director of schools and executive director of youth discipleship in his church body's international headquarters.

Each position was unique, stretching and growing Dr. Nelson's skills, faith, and ministry philosophy. They blessed him with exposure to a diversity of ages, ethnicities, socioeconomic demographics, geographic locations, and levels of synodical ministry. They also motivated Dr. Nelson to continue his education resulting in an MSEd in family studies and an EdD in leadership for the advancement of learning and service.

Though his ministry was diverse, there was a universal thread. Every place Dr. Nelson served, he was also involved with Sunday school in one way or another: teacher, superintendent, youth ministry director, national church-body executive providing services and support, and always an advocate.

Dr. Nelson has learned things that can be helpful to others. Though not comfortable being called an expert, he has experienced and studied a lot on the subject. He also found Sunday school ministry to be the thing he most loved doing.

Dr. Nelson and his wife, Carol, have been married for for-ty-four years. They have three grown and married children and seven grandchildren.

www.ingramcontent.com/pod-product-compliance
Lightning Source LLC
Chambersburg PA
CBHW071325150726
47997CB00002B/602